Asabiyya
and
State

A Reconstruction of Ibn Khaldun's Philosophy of History

KAMAL MIRAWDELI

AuthorHouse™ UK
1663 Liberty Drive
Bloomington, IN 47403 USA
www.authorhouse.co.uk
Phone: 0800.197.4150

© 2015 Kamal Mirawdeli. All rights reserved.

No part of this book may be reproduced, stored in a retrieval system, or transmitted by any means without the written permission of the author.

Published by AuthorHouse 07/09/2015

ISBN: 978-1-5049-4398-7 (sc)
ISBN: 978-1-5049-4399-4 (hc)
ISBN: 978-1-5049-4642-1-(e)

Print information available on the last page.

Any people depicted in stock imagery provided by Thinkstock are models, and such images are being used for illustrative purposes only.
Certain stock imagery © Thinkstock.

This book is printed on acid-free paper.

Because of the dynamic nature of the Internet, any web addresses or links contained in this book may have changed since publication and may no longer be valid. The views expressed in this work are solely those of the author and do not necessarily reflect the views of the publisher, and the publisher hereby disclaims any responsibility for them.

Contents

Preface 1

Part One

History And Theory: A General Introduction To Philosophy Of History

1. The Concept of History: A preliminary discourse 4
2. Time and Historical Sense 4
3. The Nature of Historical Knowledge 6
4. The Structure of Reality and the Structure of Knowledge 6
5. History and Philosophy 11
6. Meta- history and Idealist Approach 12
7. Meta- history and Scientific Method 15
8. The Science of History 20

Part Two

Ibn Khaldun's Philosophy Of History

Chapter 1   Ibn Khaldun Phenomenon: The Historical
            Conditions Of Its Possibility 31

Chapter 2   Constructing A Science Of History 38
            1.1   Foreword 38

		1.2	The Threshold 39
		1.3	Philosophy and religion 44
		1.4	Towards a scientific theory of knowledge 49
		1.1	Towards a scientific theory of history 57

Chapter 3	The Historicity Of Knowledge 62

	1.1	Man's cognitive relationship with the world 62
	1.2	The necessity of principles for understanding history. 64

Chapter 4	Knowledge And Method: The Question Of Truth 67
	4.1 The meanings of history 67
	4.2 Errors of traditional historians 69
	4.3 Change of concepts and definitions 69

Chapter 5	Man And History: The Question Of Power 77
	5.1 Philosophical premises 77
	5.2 The Historicization of the World of Existence 80
	5.3 Asabiyya and Umran 82

Chapter 6	Asabiyya And The Decline Of The State. 89
	6.1 Elements of asabiyya 89
	6.2 The internal contradiction between royal authority and asabiyya 92
	6.3 Asabiyya and Beyond: The Question of Civilization 94
	6.4 The case of Arabs 95

Chapter 7	Epilogue: The politics of Historical Thought 102

Bibliography 109
Sources: 113

Preface

The year 2006 was the 600th anniversary of the death of the greatest Arab historical thinker, Ibn Khaldun. Several events around the world were organised to commemorate the great intellectual achievements of Ibn Khaldun (1332-1406) in the fields of historiography, sociology and philosophy.

This should have been an occasion not only to commemorate Ibn Khaldun but also to initiate a serious intellectual analysis of the great gap of ignorance and darkness which has, since his death, dominated the Arab culture in particular and Islamic culture in general culminating in the transformation of Islam into an ideology of social enslavement, national repression, ignorance, and intolerance.

Ibn Khaldun was a scientific logical thinker devoid of nationalist and religious prejudices. Following the steps of Socrates and Aristotle, he turned the pursuit of knowledge into an art, and turned this art into a logical tool for rational analysis and the production of scientific knowledge representing objective truth. But this methodology was threatening enough to entrenched despotic power structures to make him despised by fundamentalists and rejected by Arab nationalist and racist "academic" institutions.

I studied philosophy of history for my MA at Essex University in 1983 and chose Ibn Khaldun for my MA dissertation. I have never had chance to revise and prepare the study for publication although a part of it (the second chapter) was published as an independent paper by the Essex University in 1984.

Being motivated by the 600 anniversary of Ibn Khaldun's death and realising the important relevance of his scientific thought to explaining even today's historical events and conditions especially in the Middle East, I revised my study and prepared this version for publication. My sole purpose is to help a better understanding of the situation of Islamic thought and the political context of events in the Middle East in the light of an epoch-making scientific theory of history produced more than 600 years ago!

Note: All the quotations from Ibn Khaldun are from Franz Rosenthal's excellent translation: The Muqaddima (3 volumes), Princeton University Press, and 2nd ed. 1967. I preferred to retain the world "asabiyya" instead of his transition of it as "group feeling" as this may not give an accurate sense of the term. Perhaps tribal solidarity is a more accurate translation. However, I prefer to keep Ibn Khaldun's original term.

Part One

History and Theory

A general introduction to philosophy of history

1. The Concept of History: A preliminary discourse

The term 'history' has a double sense or, as Raymond Aaron puts it, a double ambiguity. "In the concrete sense, the term designates a certain reality; in the formal sense, the knowledge of the reality".[1] the reality which history records and develops into a form of knowledge, as it has traditionally been understood since Aristotle, is what human beings have actually done and suffered. The double sense of the word, however, has not only created such an ambiguity which we encounter in statements such as: history repeat itself, and Tom is reading history.[2] it, in fact, problematizes the whole concept of history establishing it as an epistemological problem, i.e.: the problem of the relation between man and the world; between reality and knowledge. The historian's task can never be confined to the transcription of reality as a sequence of facts, or producing a mirror image of the event as it has really happened. Therefore, it is necessary to approach the philosophy of history in terms of the theory of knowledge. For the theory of knowledge involves a theory of reality that, by necessity, leads to a certain mode of philosophical thinking, the investigating of which helps us to grasp the mechanism of the reciprocal structure and transformation between the essential unity of the world and the essential unity of knowledge. We can start out from the face that history as a theoretical narrative construct that we develop from the historical events, implies a certain concept of time. Actions unfold in time and, therefore, the possibility of historical knowledge is not an act of mind as such. It is conditions by the possibilities of the occurrence of an event in its spatio-temprorality. Thus, involved in any historical writing, is the historian's understanding concerning the temporal pattern of the unfolding of events which, to a certain extent, articulates the pattern of his philosophical vision of the nature of those events.

2. Time and Historical Sense

The development of man's consciousness of time was in itself the product of his utilitarian cognitive relationship with the outside world. Man's first attempt to elaborate systems of chronology were associated with his awareness of time as a response to his need to procure an access to certain natural events that mysteriously occurred and recurred in time and seriously influenced his life. As Barnes states "the concept of time was produced by the consciousness of natural repetition and the necessity of differentiating between days on the basis of their particular scared virtues or qualities."[3] As the primitive man was neither able to know himself nor understand the conditions of his livelihood, his historical sense, in its mythological matrix, regarded a great variety of natural objects and events with fear or awe as manifestations of supernatural power or as its locus. And it was the deeds of gods and not men that the early calendars were originally designed to fix and record, and the early epics embraced and told. In ancient Mesopotamia, after Babylon had first established an empire "there appeared the first interpretation of history based on the very ancient view that disaster fell on any state which neglected its gods."[4] The second category which obtained historical significance, i.e.: became worthy of being the subject of historical recording, was those individuals who were associated with gods through the privilege of their wealth, power or knowledge. It was the names of the kings, and their deeds which shaped man's early "historical" records. The ancient Egyptians named the years from the reign of a particular king or by some great event which happened therein. The Babylonians chronicled events by compiling lists of kings, recording their genealogies and describing the buildings they erected. Even the elements of social history, as the Code of Hammurabi demonstrates, were incorporated into the way he organised the communal life of his subjects. In Assyria, Royal Annals were used as reliable means for dating purposes. The Assyrians also produced historical documents and chronicles that were designed to glorify Assyria and its gods and to portray the evil deeds of the wicked Babylonians.[5] What all these first Oriental attempts at elaborating a sense of time had in common was man's concern not to understand the event as such, but as a force that influenced his position and destiny in life. Hence it was power in its metaphysical and mythological manifestations which established itself as the primary object of historical consciousness.

3. The Nature of Historical Knowledge

As we approach history in terms of the theory of knowledge, it is appropriate to investigate the distinction that Aristotle makes between history and poetry: that poetry describes the things "that might happen, i.e. what is possible, probable or necessary, while the historian describes what has actually happened." Therefore, according to Aristotle, "poetry is philosophical and universal whereas the historian's statements are singular."[6]

It is true, as we have already noticed, that man's historical sense came into being in conjunction with his necessity to reflect the nature of the events that had actually happened. But what determined his view of the events was his "concern" about it, i.e. his conceiving of the events as a mysterious force that conditioned the possibilities of his very existence. That is why man expressed himself both mythologically and theologically and, being unable to understand the objective conditions of his livelihood, pointed to his conceived god's will as an explanation of the world. This implies that we can always discern in the thematic construction of historical events an ideological perspective that goes beyond the actuality of the events. Therefore, Aristotle's differentiation between history and poetry as two essentially distinct modes of knowledge is valid only as methodology. Nonetheless, his argument displays an important fact about historiography: that the nature and scope of historical knowledge is confined by its subject-matter which comprises the actual events of life, while poetry enjoys a free play on reality and thus attains more universal horizons. This point will become more substantiated when we encounter historiography as dealing not with gods and symbols of power but with actual human actions and social phenomena, with peoples and civilizations. Here we have to return to Greek historiography and investigate it in some detail. The justification of this step lies in the fact that Greek thought establishes those historical beginning of human knowledge that we cannot help having recourse to, when we intent to demonstrate truth about any given topic.

4. The Structure of Reality and the Structure of Knowledge

Greek historical writing was in the main the record of contemporary events. The Greeks failed to recover and reconstruct a remoter past. For them "history was unabashedly a preparation for life, especially political and material life."[7] Having special political concern in the events, the Greek historians wanted to understand the causes that lay behind them. Herodotus, the father of history, "begins his work by stating his purpose in writing it as to record the causes and reason for the Greek-Oriental Wars."[8] He approached these wars as the clash of two important and distant types of civilization: the Hellenic and the Oriental. Hence he embarked upon analyzing the structures of these conflicting cultures, ranging from the climates of various areas to the aspects of everyday life among the people he dealt with. He describes the diversity of peoples with unusual freedom from race prejudice. Consequently, his history is shaped as a cultural history involving a sort of descriptive sociology. But still we find that he explains the course of events in term of supernatural causation, i.e. on the basis of laws established by the gods or direct intervention of divine powers.

It was by Thucydides that for the first time in the history of human thought a materialistic interpretation of historical event was consciously attempted. Thucydides is described by Hobbes as "the most politique historiographer that ever wrote."[9] Holding a pragmatic view of history, he found that it is necessary not only to understand the external causes of historical events but also to delve into their inner or hidden causes. Ridding historical discourse of the elements of myth and fiction, he attributes historical events to rational causes and material structures. He rejects supernatural intervention in human affairs and "speaks of gods or divine powers only to show how the action of men on various occasions were influenced by belief in divine powers."[10] Thus, although both Herodotus and Thucydides take war as their object of investigation, we encounter two different theoretical approaches. Herodotus is satisfied with the supernatural interpretation of historical phenomena. Nevertheless, his metaphysical view remains super-induced and peripheral to the wide range of cultural history and topography he has produced. Thucydides' history illuminates another direction of historical knowledge. Unlike Herodotus it was not his concern to analyse the conditions of two conflicting civilizations, but to ascertain the material conditions of the Peloponnesian war, a war that shattered Greek society; a war that Thucydides, as he states in the first paragraph of his history, foresaw even at the outbreak that it would exceed any earlier conflict in significance. He describes it as the greatest upheaval ever to afflict the Greek world and involve the consciousness of every citizen in one way or another.[11] It follows, it was <u>the spirit of the age,</u> the spirit of change which unfolded itself in the phenomenon of the repetition of wars, which established an <u>epistemological challenge</u> to human thought. And Thucydides was in a position to be concerned with and able to meet this challenge. "He was the child of an age that had seen the ideal vision of a great movement of liberation fade into <u>the consciousness of mere struggle for power</u> which is to say that he lived in an age of growing imperialism when men had become jealously aware of their local advantages" Yet, Thucydides could not have grasped the magnitude of political struggle and its prognostic perspectives had he himself not been an <u>active actor</u> in the course of the contemporary events. He had been an army general and participated in some stage of the war he describes in his history as a politician he had to suffer 20 years of exile. He also lived his time intellectually, comprehending its dominant philosophical and political theories.[13] In short, his life and thought were moulded by the spirit of his age and its political and cultural manifestation. "That he was born where and when he was means that from earliest youth he had acquired that concern for problems of government which was to be the well spring of his history."[14] That is why for him history should be "a preparation for life". Although his political interest put a limitation on the scope of his thinking and the range of the knowledge he produced, it equally gave him reason to probe the deep structure of historical phenomenon, analyzing the actual and often the material aspect of the war. As a result, he arrived at a conclusion that due to "the <u>uniformity of human nature</u>", man's conflict for power would continue and such wars as the Peloponnesian war would happen again, "the reason being that, as men strove towards <u>higher material standards</u> they would find those standards impossible to attain except by means of a wider unity that would provoke war "[15] But due to the understandable narrowness of his <u>class vision</u> of the driving forces of history, he conceived of the repetition of war as a determined mechanic function of time and could not go beyond the <u>ideological frameworks</u> of the political thought of the Greek aristocracy. He assumed that "the singularly unstable from of democracy that he knew was the final and necessary form of democracy."[16].

Proceeding from a similar socio-political position as that of Thucydides, another Greek historiographer Polybius developed the interpretation of the phenomenon of the repetition of social conflict into what is known as the cyclical theory of development. By his time, the mechanics of war, the Roman war in this instance, had led to the coalescence of original societies into a single world-embracing empire, and thereby mapping historical knowledge on world scale. This situation prompted Polybius to initiate the writing of a universal history. Like Thucydides, what decided the scope and nature of his historical discourse was the spirit of the age and his own experience as an active politician. "He belonged, like Plato, to a well-to-do family with strong political connection, but for him, history not philosophy was the proper study for a future ruler."[17] In some parts of his work, he was writing history in which he himself had acted.

He called his 'Histories' "pragmatic", meaning that the historian should deal primarily with political and military matters. Polybius explicitly states that his unique attempt to write a universal history was a response to what the spirit of his age demanded, and at the same time, facilitated "For who, he wrote, "among men is so worthless or indolent as not to know how, and by subjection to what kind of constitution, the whole world came under Roman dominion in less than 53 years?"[18]

This is the epistemological challenge that his time put forward and Polybius was shrewd enough to undertake it and try to provide an explanation for it by writing his world history and elaborating his theory of the cyclic development of history. He formulates this theory in terms of the changes that take place in the constitutional formation of the state. The first form of the state is monarchy because it comes naturally as it depends on the rule of the strongest. Gradually this improves into a real kingship by a process of construction and reform because ideas of justice and virtue, which man because of his faculty of reason can develop, take root. The kingship degenerates into tyranny when a king monopolizes power and wealth and insists that his word is law. But the best people revolt against him and abolish his tyranny. As a result, aristocracy comes into being. This also degenerates into oligarchy, and the unjust rule of the oligarchs drives people to upraise and establish democracy. Democracy too degenerates into lawlessness and anarchy. Things go from bad to worse and the "mob", again reduced to an uncivilized state, finds a 'master' and the process starts again.

Polybius came to the conclusion that even Rome would not escape the tendency to fall into decline. He conceived of the cyclic development as a part of the determined order of nature. He says

"It naturally requires to be proved that all things are subject to change and decay. The inevitable processes of nature are enough to convince us on that point. Now there are two causes by which every kind of constitution may be brought to destruction. One <u>external,</u> the other arising <u>within</u>. There is no regular method of investigating the external causes but there is of the internal"[19]

The method he formulates is to account for the decline of human construction in term of the degeneration of morality and social order caused by economical prosperity.

Polybius asserts that his theoretical construction of history is based upon deriving the laws of fortune from the laws of nature. In an important passage, which I would like to quote-below, he demonstrates how the nature of his work-is decided by the reciprocal structure of the world and knowledge: he says

"The coincidence by which all the transactions of the world have been oriented in a single direction and guided towards a single goal is the extraordinary characteristic of the present age which the special feature of the present work is a corollary. <u>The unity of events imposes upon the historian a similar unity of composition</u> in depicting for his reader <u>the operation of the laws of fortune</u> upon the grand scale, and this has been my own principal inducement and stimulus in the work which I have undertaken."[20]

In fact, Polybius's account of his theory displays the mechanism of the construction of historical knowledge in Greek historiography as a whole: the mechanism which expresses itself in the unity and direction of the events, and "the unity of composition", i.e. man's intellectual capture of the apparent laws of historical process. However, what the Greek historians were mainly concerned with was the world of war, politics and great state and not a social structure undergoing the phenomena that they dealt with.

Hence, their interpretation of history remained mechanistic, reading the laws of nature as such, into the laws of social development, ending with a fatalistic view of the process of historical development. Nevertheless, their commitment to reality had a great scientific significance. It allowed historical thought to elaborate quasi-scientific procedures, move to analytical mechanisms and penetrate behind the surface structure of the events.

5. History and Philosophy

Now, let us ask: what is the position of historical knowledge in the context of philosophy?

Once we shift into the realm of philosophy we find ourselves confronted with the problematic dualism of idea/reality, or the ideal/material, as it has been philosophically and systematically constructed by Plato, with emphasis on the priority, universality, necessity, eternity, authenticity and authority of the idea. Aristotle retains this dichotomy when he classifies sciences in his Ethical Nicomachea [21] into three categories: the theoretical sciences, which include physics, mathematics and metaphysics (philosophy), the practical science and the productive sciences. According to this division, history cannot belong in the theoretical sciences because it deals with individual (particular) events that occur in a specific spatio-temporality and, thus, lacks the characteristics of the theoretical science, the proper object of which is "necessary, eternal and universal" principles "from which syllogism proceeds". For the same reason Hegel refuses to incorporate Greek historiography within his notion of philosophy of history. He classified Greek historians under the original historians.

"Whose descriptions are for the most part limited to deeds, events, and states of society, which they had before their eyes, and whose spirit they shared. They simply transformed what was passing in the world around them, to the realm of re-preventative intellect. An external phenomenon is thus translated into an internal conception."[22]

Thus, for both Aristotle and Hegel, the attachment of historical discourse to reality deprives it of entering the realm of philosophy's universal discourse. In other words, in order that history should attain a philosophical status, it must detach itself from its subject-matter and start out from idea or theory. That is to say only meta-history can establish a philosophy of history.

So far we can distinguish <u>four moments</u> in <u>the mode of the theoretical production of historical knowledge:</u>

1. Reality or the concrete: i.e. Objects, things, deeds, events, states of society as the are.
2. The transcription of (the above) reality.
3. The theoretical construction that the historian develops in the narrative structure of his writing and/or from his own interpretation of historical process.
4. Meta-history 1: (Reason, Essence, Absolute, Mind, First Intellect... etc.) as an absolute entity that exists anterior to reality.
   2: Laws and principles of interpretation or reconstruction of history.

Within these four elements the problem of the production of historical knowledge unfolds itself in terms of what has turned out to be an eternal historical struggle between idealism and materialism. According to materialism idea (or the fourth moment) is the outcome of a progressive historical and rational development of the three preceding moments. Therefore, principles and premises are, according to materialism, only scientific-units included and abstracted from man's cognitive relation with the world. While idealism reverses the process and sanctions the absolute self-existence of the idea.

6. Meta- history and Idealist Approach

Religious thought lies in the heart of the idealist concept of history. Hegel's philosophy of history, itself, is based on the Christian interpretation of providential history.[23] "Both in the Judaic and in Christian traditions, history was seen as part of a divine plan in which the actions of people and of nations were conceived".[24].

Most western discussions of the meaning or significance of history derive from there Judaic and Christian principles rather than from Greek philosophy.[25] The Christian concept of history received its final and decisive expression in St. Augustine's city of God which, as Toynbee sees it, serves as an example of a classical work of metahistory[26] [in its idealist sense]. To St. Augustine the whole process of history is providential, but he did not think that the design of divine providence had been revealed to mankind; he considered it presumptuous to profess to know what God has not revealed. Therefore, although St. Augustine, as Toynbee says:

"Released the later Hellenic world from the belief in Man's enslavement to a wholly arbitrary fate or fortune, he accomplished this at the apparent price of re-subjecting Man to the tyranny of unknowable Divine will."[27]

However St. Augustine's idealist principles could not hinder history and the spirit of the age from rereading their own image of reality; an image which Augustine had no choice but to present in his history as the earthly city or profane history in contrast to what he calls the city of God. He analyzes the mundane conditions of the decline of the Roman Empire and attribute all the causes of corruption to the evils of the city of Man in order to prove that only man's belongingness to the divine city saves his civilization from disintegration and decay.

This idealist dichotomization of history continued to dominate western thought throughout the Middle Ages, when historical thought was shaped chiefly by the feudal-church ideology, explaining historical events as the result of the intervention of the divine and as the realization of the providential plan. The Medieval historians, mostly monks, based their histories, as a rule, on annalistic accounts which lacked the elements of causation, reflection or analysis. The period, as a German historian describes it:

"Possessed no idea of historical judgement, no sense of historical reality, no trace of critical reflection. The principle of authority ruling without limitation in the religious domain, defended all tradition as well as traditional dogmas."[28]

It goes without saying that the impoverishment of historical thought in the medieval period was the natural reflection of the static spirit and backwardness of feudalism. But within this dark point of history, was the light of another civilization: that of Islam. This had entered its declining stage in the Islamic west: Spain and North Africa. In it, the greatest leap that historical thought ever achieved was found in Ibn Khaldun's Muqaddima. "Ibn Khaldun's star, at Toynbee puts it, shines the more brightly by contrast with the foil of darkness against which it flashes out."[29] (We shall discuss the Islamic concept of history and Ibn Khaldun's work in the next two parts.)

To conclude, meta-history in its idealistic sense, notwithstanding its religious or philosophical garments, is, in its essence, a class idealistic ideology, which has established itself by maintaining the gap of man's primitive ignorance, i.e.: the failure of the masses to understand the objective conditions of their life, especially the conditions of production, and to control them; the failure which deepened their sense of alienation from the world they were making. It is a class ideology because it sanctions men's ignorance and debility. It legitimizes the authority of the few and denies the ability of the people to understand the laws of history and determine their destiny. It isolates man's consciousness from his political life and rifts and essential unity between reality and idea, establishing them as two separate modes of existence. Hence, the idealist concept of history segments the totality of human life into differentiated independent domains, to be reflected upon and studied in isolation from each other. It asserts men's spirituality, egoism and pseudo-individuality. But it denies the social and political responsibilities of the individual. For example even the Christian moral ideal, love, is individual rather than social "Its primary concern is not the establishment of justice in society, but purity in the life of the individual."[30]

To repudiate the basic premises of the idealist concept of history is the independence of idea from reality or philosophy from history, it is sufficient to have a quick investigation of its own historical and political mission. First, philosophy did not come into existence in a vacuum. It did not emanate from a metaphysical space which had no relation to human reality. Hegel himself derives his idealistic principles from historical reality. Let us return to the Greeks again. The historical context of Greek thought explicitly propounds the essential unity of human knowledge. We shall mention just a few examples. The idea of causation which appeared in the historical writings of Herodotus and Thucydides had already been known in philosophy and science. Democritus in his atomistic philosophy elaborated the notion of necessity, i.e.: the unbreakable law of causality that governs everything.³¹ Also their politicization of the historical process reflected the rife ideas of Greek political philosophy.³² in his climatic interpretation of culture, Herodotus was influenced by the famous Greek physician <u>Hippocrates</u>. Polybius's cyclic of social evolution was modelled on Aristotle's theory of evolution developed from his biological studies. Owing to the permanent significant position of this idea, in the context of man's historical thought I would like to rewrite below Kurt Van Fritz's explicit account of it:

> "..... The evolution of living beings starts with comparatively simple and primitive state and then develops gradually to state of ever greater differentiation and perfection. But when the evolving form has reached a certain degree of comparative perfection which we call maturity, it continues in that state for a limited period of time, then begins to decay and finally dies. In the meantime, however, other living beings have started the same process. In other words according to this concept of evolution, the world does not develop as a whole, but remains the same while <u>within the world,</u> living beings and certain production of human civilization develop and after some time decay and die, in an everlasting circle."³³

The foregoing instances exemplify the unity of human knowledge on the basis of its vital relation to historical reality.

The second point which I want to elucidate briefly is the partisanship of philosophy. Every philosophy comes into existence in response to a social demand. Every so-called impartial interpretation of history is, in the last analysis subservient to the interests of specific class or dominant world view. This is a pattern characteristic of philosophical thought throughout history. Socrates, Plato and Aristotle for instance, had been theorizers of the Greek aristocracy before being philosophers as such.

7. Meta- history and Scientific Method

Radical transformations in man's historical thought are always linked with great historical transmutation in the structure of society. As a rule, the tendency of historical thought towards <u>scientificity</u> depends on the extent of man's scientific progress in general, and his political awareness in particular. It is the latter that allows man to view the totality of events in their relation to a central structure which is man's political existence, proceeding from which he can get rid of the dichotomies of idealist philosophy and, instead, get at scientific generalizations

The European humanist historiography of the Renaissance in the 15th and 16th centuries marked the first stage in the development of bourgeoisie historical thought, which unfolded in breaking with feudal-theological interpretation of the world and reviving the political thought of Greek historiography and philosophy. In Italy, <u>Nicola Machiavelli</u> (1469-1527) transferred humanist historiography into a modern political scholarship.[35] although he was primarily concerned with state-utilitarianism, he actually worked a philosophy of history into it, by attempting to grasp the nature of historical causation in its political aspects and present a clear image of the process of historical development. Therefore, he could bring to history a genuine inductive method. He taught that a statesman should make an empirical study of actual men and the causes generally at work in the life of the state. His theory of the state, however, was not original. It "went back to Aristotle and the fifth book of his politics"[36] Also, Machiavelli renewed the cyclical theory of socio-political development.

In France, the Enlightenment advanced rational historiography founded by <u>Voltaire</u> and <u>Montesquieu</u>. Theorizing the free development of bourgeoisie culture and prosperity, Voltaire replaced the idealist dogmatic dualism of idea versus reality by a new discourse formation: viz. Reason/unreason. "He looked upon human history as having been carried along chiefly by the clash of ideas and civilizations. Christianity challenged paganism, Mohammadianism came into conflict with Christianity."[37] He argued that the three major forces which moved the minds of men are climate, government and religion.

<u>Montesquieu</u> continued the line of thought established by Machiavelli and broadened the idea of statesmanship into the art of the lawgiver,

embracing all social and human need as far as it had any connection with the state. He saw climate as the most powerful cause of the difference in the human race, and in so doing he viewed history first and foremost in terms of its physical conditions,[38] adapting an extreme collectivist and fatalistic interpretation of history. However, the transition of Europe from a traditional to a modern industrial society was concomitant with a new secular idea of scientific and social progress which allowed history to achieve a high level of rational perception and a more advanced methodology that ever before. But philosophy of history still remained as the "third moment" or as the first order enquiry, i.e., as interpretation of historical event, and not as the means by which facts and interpretations could be constructed, i.e., as scholarship.

Therefore, as Arthur Marwick puts it, "Voltaire and his contemporaries might best be regarded as standing, not so much at the beginning of a new historical tradition but at the highest point of an old one. For history in the final sense, history as a scholarly discipline begins only with Ranke [**Leopold von Ranke** (1795 –1886)] and his German compatriots at the beginning of the nineteenth century."[39]

At this stage of the development of historical thought, we have to speak of a new notion of the philosophy of history, or metahistory. Now we have the philosophy of history as a second order enquiry, to use the expression of the Encyclopaedia Britannica, "whose attention is focused upon the procedures and categories used by practicing historians in approaching their material."[40] This level of philosophy of history is generally known as critical or analytical philosophy of history. This suggests that the philosophy of history starts out from what we have called "the fourth epistemological moment", from metahistorical principles, not in the sense of Absolute Idea but in the sense of scientific principles and laws induced from the march of history itself. For in order that history should become a science, we, inevitably, need principles and abstract generalization to start out from, acquired by means of a comprehensive study of the sum total of accumulated historical data. In this respect, Lenin says: "The gathering of facts about various events, phenomena and processes is one aspect of history as a science. On the basis of an analysis of the totality of facts, history grasps the essence of individual phenomena and processes in the life of society and discovers not only the specific laws of its development of individual countries and peoples, in comparison with other countries and peoples. <u>History expresses</u> all such discoveries in the form of <u>theoretical generalizations.</u>"[41]

It is only then the historian consciously constructs his method of approach, <u>i.e.:</u> his principle and beginnings in terms of historical scholarship. Until the nineteenth century, no one except for <u>Ibn-Khaldun</u> and <u>Vico</u> had elaborated a comprehensive scientific historiography.

Giambattista Vico's attempt in this respect is very outstanding. Vico, as a brilliant thinker, "Set himself the task of formulating the principles of historical method... a principle by which to distinguish what can be known from what cannot; a doctrine of the necessary limits of human knowledge."[42] The principle which he formulates is that man can only know and understand what he himself has made. Hence, Vico counterpoised <u>Descartes</u> thesis that the criterion of truth is idea and that the world of nature, to which the methods of mathematical physics are applicable, is the most appropriate object of scientific study. Instead, Vico suggests that "The world of nature, which since god made it, he alone knows", therefore, the right object of science is "The civil world, the world of nature, as it has been made by men."[43] The rule and criterion of truth is, then, to Vico, to have made it. "Hence the idea of the mind not only cannot be the criterion of other truths, but it cannot be the criterion of the mind itself, for while the mind apprehends itself, it does not make itself; it is ignorant of the form or mode by which it apprehends itself."[44]

The thrust of Vico's new science lies in elaborating a new concept as to the <u>subject-matter</u> of history, which is the construction of civil society. Concomitant with this concept, Vico also formulates the principle of his method: that every theory "must begin where its subject matter began".[45] That is, its beginnings.

Then, where can we find the historical beginnings of civil society?

Not from the points where the philosophers began to reflect on human ideas, Vico answers, but "from the time when men began to think humanly"[46], i.e.: when human savagery was followed by social organization. Vico's point of departure with western philosophy's disjunction between spirit and life and the ancient disjunction between idea and image lies in his approach to "the beginnings" by way of a new theory of knowledge. The basis of Vico's originality is his conception of <u>fantasia</u> on which he builds his philosophy. "Through his discovery of the imaginative universal, of fantasia as a way of thinking and acting, Vico, according to Donald Philip Vevene, finds a new origin for philosophical thought".[47]

Applying fantasia to the discovery of the beginnings of human institutions Vico decides these principles:

1. The first founders of civil society were not philosophers, but man-beasts devoid of culture and humanity yet guided by an observe instinct of fear and self-preservation to "something superior to nature ... the light of God".[48] Men in the "bestial state of being" under <u>the tyranny of self-love</u>, which made the fulfilment of egoistic desires the only way to the widening of the circle of human association, could not develop social institutions (family, tribe, town, nation) without creating the notion of God: the first step of the humanisation of man-beasts. "In order of its principal aspects, this science must therefore be a rational civil theology of divine providence"[49]
2. Once the notion of providence had made the establishment of civil society possible, Man began to <u>think</u> of the necessities or utilities of social life. The second aspect of the science, accordingly, should be "A history of human ideal, on which it seems the metaphysics of human mind must proceed."[50]
3. But history of ideas unfolds itself in time and place. Therefore, the New Science has to narrate "this ideal eternal history" as "traversed in time by the history of every notion in its rise, development maturity, decline, and fall"[51]

Thus, Vico presupposes a cycle of development in the historical process of every nation. He thinks of this cycle as a parallel to the evolution of human nature and his economic demands. "The natures of people" is, according to him, "First crude, then serve, then benign, then delicate, finally dissolute. And the sequences of man's demands are first, necessity, then utility, then comfort, then pleasures, then luxury and finally mad extravagance."[52]

Although Vico establishes his science as the history of idea, as an ideal eternal history, to him, as <u>Collingwood</u> remarks "There is no antithesis between the historic action of men and the divine plan that holds the together as there was for t Middle Ages."[53] He considered the historical laws themselves to be providential "Since, he says, "In God knowledge and creation is one and the same thing."[54] (This concept is almost identical to the Islamic concept of knowledge.)[55] Hence, Vico's science is characterised by a genuine historicism which allows him to develop an integrate interpretation of language, art, religion, law and the form of socio-economical formation in their interrelationship and unity of historical development. Moreover

"He saw for the first time how history and philosophy, the science of universals and the research into every sort of practical fact, need not remain two separate forms of knowledge, merely juxtaposed or opposed but might be united to constitute a system of universal law."[56]

By establishing the fact that the world of history and society, unlike the realm of nature, is man-made, Vico, for the first time in the history of western thought, made man: his institutions, societies, nations, his customs, his laws, forms of social and economic organization, language, religion, etc. the genuine subject-matters of historiography.

However, building his philosophy on <u>fantasia</u>, Vico allowed a lot of myth to enter his history. He failed to work out scientific laws of social development. Instead, he believed that purely 'philosophical' proofs of general historical and theological 'truths', established by his science, are possible.

8. The Science of History

A comprehensive materialistic concept of history was worked out in the nineteenth century by Marx and Engels. This concept, known as historical materialism, tries to put an end to the dualism of 'the world of men' and 'the world of nature' as well as to all one-sided evaluations of certain factories in historical development. Pre-Marxist materialist views of the world, in general, had confined themselves to the understanding of nature elevating to an absolute the laws of natural science in simplified metaphysical, mechanistic forms. Therefore, they had failed to elaborate a materialistic interpretation of socio-economic life or signal a fundamental break with idealism. Lenin, defining the position and nature of Marx's achievement, says:

> "At best, pre-Marxist 'sociology' and historiography brought forth an accumulation of new facts, collected at random, and a description of individual aspects of the historical process. By examining the <u>totality</u> of opposing tendencies, by reducing them to precisely <u>definable conditions</u> of life and production of the various <u>classes</u> of society, by discarding subjectivism and arbitrariness in the choice of particular "dominant idea or in its interpretation, and by revealing that, without exception, all ideas and all the various tendencies stem from <u>'the conditions of the materials forces of production'</u>, Marxism indicated the way to an <u>all-embracing and comprehensive study</u> of the process of the rise, development and decline of socio-economic systems."[57]

By establishing the principle of the unity of the world on the basis of its materiality, Marxism completely reversed the idealist concept of history and founded the basis of a comprehensive revolution in all the aspect of human thought and life.

Marxism, itself did not come into being in isolation from the mainstream of development of historical and scientific thought. Lenin expounding the cultural context of Max's idea wrote.
"Marx was the genius who continued and completed the three chief ideological currents of the 19th century, respectively by the three most advanced centuries of humanity: classical German philosophy, classical

English political economy and French socialism combined with French revolutionary doctrines."[58]

The greatest achievement of Marx, by means of which he established the fundamentals of Maxims, was the unification of dialectics with materialism. In this achievement, Marx based himself on <u>Hegel</u> and <u>Feuerbach</u>. It is noteworthy that these two philosophers, in their turn "constantly addressed themselves to the question first contained implicitly in the works of Bacon and Descartes: how can man <u>rationally</u> dominate nature and manage society?"[59] Despite being an idealist, Hegel developed the dualism of nature /spirit into a dialectical doctrine of historical process. He says:

> "The history of the world begins with its general aim-the realization of the idea of spirit-only in an <u>implicit</u> form (an such) that is, as nature; a hidden, most profoundly hidden, unconscious instinct; and the whole process of history... is directed to rendering this unconscious impulse a conscious one."[60]

Hegel's point of departure was that development is conditioned by the contradiction not as anomaly, but in term of the interaction of oppositions, as the principle of all <u>self-motive</u>. The rational kernel of Hegel's dialects which Marx discerned and developed was the concept of universality, essentiality and necessity of development, which according to Hegel, takes place through the emergence and overcoming of internal contradictions, the mutual transaction of opposites, the leap-like transaction of quantitative into qualitative changes, the negation of the old by the new.

Also, Marx integrated into his philosophy <u>Feuerbach's</u> anthropological materialism, which construers thought as a natural human ability, inseparable from the brain, from the physical organisation, and indissolubly connected with the sensory reflection of the external material world. Feuerbach regarded man as the highest expression of nature, through whom nature feels, thinks and realizes itself. He saw gregariousness, the desire to sociality, as an essential part of man's nature. But Feuerbach failed to understand the essence of human society and the laws of its development because he regarded human association merely, as a matter of love and spiritual affinity. In his Thesis on Feuerbach, Marx criticizes him for his failure to see religious sentiment itself as a social product, and his abstracting human "essence" from historical process.[61] In fact, in his concept of history, namely the role of social practice, Marx asserts that it is only in the context of human action that the problematic dichotomy of subject and object can be overcome. "The question whether objective truth can be attributed to human thinking ..which is isolated from practice is a purely scholastic question.

"The materialist doctrine that men are products of circumstances and upbringing, and that, therefore, changed men are products of other circumstances and changed upbringing, forgets that it is men that change circumstances and that the educator himself needs education,... The coincidence of the changing circumstances and of human activity can be conceived and rationally understood only as revolutionary practice"[62]

The crucial position of the question of praxis in Marx's thought does not lie only in its repudiation of the basic thesis of classical bourgeoisie philosophy that the attainment of the dominance of man over the forces of nature and society by means of reason alone is possible, but also in determining the nature of his philosophy as a radical ideology providing a revolutionary programme for political action. Marx's own revolutionary practice among the proletariat and his penetrating political insight into the revolutionary events of the end of the 18th and the first half of the 19th centuries testified to his view that class struggle was the most important driving force in historical development. In fact, Marx, notwithstanding previous achievements in philosophical and scientific thought, would not have been able to formulate his all-embracing materialistic theory of history without finding his point of departure for theoretical and political action in adapting the position, needs and interests of the most impoverished and most revolutionary rising class of his time, which had so far been denied any role in shaping history, namely, the working class. It was at the heart of the interest of this class, which according to him had nothing to lose but its fetters, to lay bare all the aspects and elements of social reality in their interconnection and contradictions, with a view to changing history. Hence, the possibility of discovering the real objective law of social development, from which Marx, synthesizing materialism and dialectics, formed his science of history.

Marx and Engels wrote:

> "We know only a single science, the science of history. One can look at history from two sides and divide it into the history of nature and the history of man. Those two sides are, however, inspirable. The history of nature and the history of men are dependent on each other so long as men exist."[63]

Footnotes

PART 1

(1) Raymond Aaron: Introduction to the Philosophy of History: tr. By. G.J. Irwin, London, 1960. P. 15

(2) See: Patrick Gardiner: The Nature of Historical Explanation Oxford, 1980. Pp. Xi-x

(3) Harry Elmer Barnes: A History of Historical Writing) Dover publication, New York, 1963. P. 12 (Hereafter: Barnes)

(4) Herbert Butterfields: Historiography in Dictionary of the History of ideas
New York, 1973. V. 2, p. 465 (Hereafter: Butterfields)

(5) See: Barnes op. Cit. Pp. 13-14
(6) Aristotle: Art of poetry
Tr. W. Hamilton Fyfe, Oxford, 1940. P. 25
(7) Arthur Marwick: The Nature of History
Macmillan, 1970. P. 26
(8) Kurt von Fritz: The of ideas in Ancient Greek historiography in Dictionary of the History of Ideas p. 501 (Hereafter: Fritz)
(9) Hobbes: Thucydides: of the life and History p. 172
(10) Fritz: op. Cit. P. 501
(11) (11) Thucydides: Peloponnesian War
Tr. Richard Cravenly, every Man's Library, London, 1914. Book I, ch. I, p. 1-16
(12) John H. Finley: Thucydides
Ann Arbore, 1963. P. 54 (Hereafter: Finley)
(13) See: Finley op. Cit. (Thucydides) Intellectual Background pp. 36-73
(14) Ibid p. 34-35
(15) Ibid p. 291-292
(16) Ibid p. 319

(17) T.A Sinclair: A History of Greek Political thought, London, 1967. P. 272
(18) Polybius: the Histories, Tr... By. W. R. Paton, Harvard University press, 1975. Book I, V, I, P. 3-4
(19) Cited in Sinclair: A History of Greek Political Thought p. 274
(20) Polybius: The histories: Book I, chs. 1-4
(21) Aristotle: Ethica Nicomachea Book VI, 3-9. In The Works of Aristotle tr. By. W. D. Ross Oxford University press, 1963, Vol. IX
(22) Hegel: The Philosophy of History tr. By J. Sibree, New York, 1944. Pp. 1-2ion
(23) E.H Gomrich argues that at Hegel's philosophy of history is "an extension, or possibly a perversion of the Christian interpretation of providential history." See: Gombrich: In Search cultural History Caledon presses, 1969. Pp. 8-14
(24) Ibid, p.8
(25) See: The New Encyclopaedia Britannica (1974) v. 8 "Historiography". Theological Origins p. 962
(26) Arnold Toynbee: A study of History Oxford, 1972. P. 487
(27) Ibid p. 488
(28) Cited in Barnes. Op. Cit. Pp. 56-57
(29) Toynbee: A Study of History Oxford, v. 3, p. 321
(30) See: Reinhold Niebuhr: "Christian politics and communist Religion" in "Christianity and social Revolution" Ed. By John Lewis, London, 1935. Pp. 442-460
(31) Fritz: op. Cit. Pp. 505-506
(32) See: Finley: op. Cit. The thought of Thucydides pp. 289-325
(33) Fritz: op. Cit. Pp. 505-506
(34) Ellen Meiskins Wood and Neal Wood: class Ideology and Ancient Political Theory Oxford, 1970. pp. 1-5
(35) See Barnes: pp. 107-110
(36) Friedrich Meinecke: Historicism, tr. By J. E. Anderson-Rutledge and Kegan Paul, London, 1972, p. 97 (in comparison with Montesquieu)
(37) Barnes: p. 154
(38) Barnes: p. 154
(39) Meinecke: op. Cit. 70
(40) Arthur Marwick: The Nature of History p. 25

(41) New Encyclopaedia Britannica (1974): (philosophy of) History. P. 961
(42) R.G. Collingwood: The Idea of History Oxford, 1962. P. 64
(43) Cited in Great Soviet Encyclopaedia: (V. 10) History p. 98
(44) The New Science of Giambettista Vico tr. By Thomas Goddard Bergin and Max Harold Frisch Anchor books, 1961, units 331-332 (p. 52-53) (Hereafter The New Science)
(45) See: Max Harold Frisch and Thomas Goddard Bergin (Introduction to) The Autobiography of Giamabattista Vico Conrad University press, 1944. Pp. 38-49 and 57)
(46) Ibid 338
(47) See: D.P. Verne: "Vico's originality" in his Vico's Science of Imagination, Cornell University press, 1981. Pp. 17-35
(48) The New Science: 338/339
(49) Ibid 342, 385
(50) Ibid 347
(51) Ibid 349
(52) lXVI: 241 XLVII: 242
(53) Collingwood: The Idea of history
(54) The new Science: 349
(55) See: Part II of this dissertation
(56) Max Harold Frisch: op. Cit. P. 40
(57) V.I Lenin: Marx, Engels, Marxism London, 1931. P. 13
(58) Lenin: The teaching of Karl Marx New York international publishers, 1973. V. I. P. 101 see also: Lenin "The Three Sources and three component part of Marxism" in no. 57 pp. 50-55
(59) Manfrea Buhr: "The greatness and Limitations of classical bourgeois philosophy" in Soviet studies in Philosophy Spring, 1975. P.73
(60) Hegel: The philosophy of History
(61) Marx: Theses on Feuerbach in Marx, Engels, Lenin "On historical Materialism" progress publishers, Moscow, 1972
(62) Ibid Theses 2 and 3
(63) Cited in Great Soviet Encyclopaedia. History p. 98 see also: Marx and Engels: <u>The German Ideology:</u>
1) History pp. 39-48
2) Concerning the production of consciousness pp. 49-54

Part Two

IBN KHALDUN'S PHILOSOPHY OF HISTORY

Chapter One

IBN KHALDUN PHENOMENON: THE HISTORICAL CONDITIONS OF ITS POSSIBILITY

The constituent elements of historical thought can be identified as follows:

1. The spirit of the age, i.e.: the direction that time imposes on the course of human life and the challenging problems it brings forwards.
2. The political, social and intellectual position of the historian in regard to his age.
3. The dominant ideological framework, i.e.: the political orientation of thought with a view to perpetuating the power structure of the state.
4. Tradition.

It is these elements that determine the range, nature and quality of human thought in any historical epoch.

The challenging problems of Ibn Khaldun's were manifest in more than one field. They were a complex of political, social and intellectual problems.

But Ibn Khaldun was in a position not only to be conscious of and concerned with them, but also to approach them and philosophise them in terms of their historical unity. The narrative of his life is too well-known to need any further investigation. Therefore, we shall confine ourselves to the indication of those hallmarks that help us to account for the deep insight into social phenomena, which he unfolds in the Muqaddima.

Ibn Khaldun was born in Tunis on May 27th, 1332. Since the tenth century, his family, Khaldun, had become famous for leadership in revolutionary activities in Seville, and, once a young man, Ibn Khaldun found himself deeply involved in the political life characterizing the historical course of his family.

Early in his life, he engaged actively in political affairs and showed an intense interest in revolutionary change in North Africa and Muslim Spain, where he served a successive number of rulers as a general, a political adviser, and once as a prime minister. Then, he had to participate in, suffer from, and witness the greatest events of his ages. He was in Egypt in the time of the Mongol invasion. He was in Damascus while Tamerlane besieged it and his interview with the conqueror is one of the most interesting episodes of history. His political activities always ended in disaster. Intellectually, Ibn Khaldun had absorbed all the learning accessible to a statesman of his time. He had memorized all the Quran and familiarized himself with the masterpieces of Arabic literature. He was a master of religious learning, an outstanding jurisprudent, and a writer in logic. He was especially interested in the Islamic Law and Greek Political Philosophy.

Against this background we shall study his approach to the problems dictated by the spirit of his ages; the problems which theoretically speaking, can be represented in two phenomena:

1. The contradiction between the Sharia and political reality.

2. The contradiction between Revelation, i.e.: the Quranic principles, and Reason or Philosophy.

The contradiction between the Sharia, as the embodiment of the Islamic political system, and reality, which started soon after Muhammad's death, had been exacerbated by the vicissitudes of political life throughout centuries of Islamic rule. This contradiction culminated in Ibn Khaldun's time in the decline and decay of the Islamic State, and consequently Islamic civilization. If Muslim civilization in other parts of the world had been in decline, in North Africa where Ibn Khaldun lived, it had virtually ceased to exist. Muhsin Mahadi rightly states that:

"The desire to understand the nature and causes of the conditions prevailing in the Islamic world, and particularly in North Africa, during his life time, and to learn the lessons they could teach him on the nature of human history, were among the main motivations in Ibn Khaldun's reflection of history." (Mahdi, 26)

However, his desire to reflect on history was not an abstract one. It was through his own tragedy that Ibn Khaldun entered the realm of history, knocking at its great gate, hoping to hear consolatory echoes of his own disaster. His mind being both religiously and politically shaped, Ibn Khaldun believed that the Sharia was the best safeguarding basis of a united and rational community. Hence, following Plato, he placed the historical significance on the ruler, regarding him as "the soul of the community", who must be in complete control of the State. It was enough for the ruler, Ibn Khaldun thought, to be wise and act according to the Law and philosophical norms in order to be able to safeguard the stability of the state and the unity of umma (nation). But this understanding led to nothing but his own victimization.

"He was successively an advisor to the ruler of Marocco, a teacher who tried to impart philosophy to the ruler of Granada, and prime minister in Bijaya. These efforts ended in complete failure." (ibid)

He could see ever-persisting struggle for power, which had been taking place everywhere. In Spain he could see the ruins left by centuries of

Muslim and Christian warfare. He reflected that even the Caliphate, which he considered the best form of royal authority, had also been vulnerable to decline and decay. Civilization, which for Ibn Khaldun, proved to be the best consequence of man's rational and social activities had generated nothing, as his experience in Egypt had demonstrated for him, except for moral corruption and social disintegration. All these facts and phenomena made Ibn Khaldun realize that there are some objective conditions and "hidden laws" that restrain history from proceeding in conformity with religious laws and philosophical norms.

Hence his recourse to history, to the studying of the actual conditions and particular circumstances of historical events; to learn their lessons and work out from them a new insight into historical process, a new philosophy of life. Hence, the title of his historical works- "The Book of Historical Lessons" But approaching history as the locus of *ibar*, lessons, in itself, necessitates applying a new method for both distinguishing and designating these lessons on the one hand, and understanding and assessing their truth, on the other.

As the question of "understanding" and "truth" are essentially epistemological questions, Ibn Khaldun had to tackle them in terms of their universality.

Hence, his brilliant intellectual initiative that marks a historical break in the process of human thought: his recourse to philosophy and its universal principles in order to work out a scientific method of historical approach, as we shall explain in the next chapter.

The second challenging problem was a cultural one: the problem of the contradiction between religion and philosophy. What initiated this problem was the discrepancy that frequently appeared in different interpretations of the Quranic verses. The first encounter of Islam with Greek Philosophy in the second century of Hijra (9th century A.D) resulted in the rationalization of this problem. The Mu'tazilites were the first Muslim Mutakallimun, speculative theologians, who emerged through controversies involving the interpretations of the Quran in its anthropomorphic description of God and denial of human volition. They rejected literary interpretation of the Quranic passages and affirmed free will, while the Orthodox traditionalists adhered to Literalism and determinism. In response to the rational challenge of Greek philosophy, they chose to defend the Islamic faith by the use of reason, emphasizing, as Ibn Khaldun explains, two Islamic principles: first, "al-tauhid": the declaration of the oneness of God; according to which they affirmed God's possession of the attributes of divinity and perfection as "abstract data of mind", but did not assume the existence of a divine attribute persisting in the divine essence.

Second, adl, justice, according to which they considered it is God's duty to observe what is best for mankind". (Al-Muqaddima, V. III, p. 61-2) Originally, they denied predestination and rejected Tabary's claim that history cannot be rationally investigated. At the end of the third century, the dominance of Mutazilite Kalam in Sunni circles was challenged and replaced by Asharism (the name of the school is derived from its originator Abul-Hassan al-Ashari) which, in its process, devoted itself to defend the Orthodox traditionalism against philosophy, following the method of argument and, in fact, philosophising Kalam itself without jeopardizing the Quranicdogmas and the Islamic ethos. Thus they emphasized the paramountcy of religious dogmas. Starting from what they considered as the articles of faith they formulated a rational system based upon principles and method of proof, which led to conclusion identical with these dogmas. (See Ibn Khaldun V. III, p. 144-7).

They argued against the notion of secondary causality, contending that all we perceive is the succession of events, not any causal chain between them.

"They believed that there is no substantial continuity, between things as well as between moments of time and points of space. The whole cosmic matrix was segmented and atomized. To fulfil the gap the Asharite appealed to Divine Will. For them, it is the Divine Will which relates two moments of existence together and gives homogeneity to the world above us."

Being ideologically subservient to the interests of the political system, Asharism was officially adopted as the recognized school of the Islamic doctrine in 1055.

"It has continued to be dominant to this day. It became the arch opponent of philosophy (falsafa) and all the theosophical and philosophical schools that were based on a systematic and rational – although not rationalistic – approach to knowledge."

Thus Asharism has become the dominant worldview in the Islamic world especially after philosophy had received from Al-Ghazali, the greatest proponent of Kalam, and the most influential theologian that has ever appeared in Islam, a deadly blow that it has never recovered from in the Islamic East. It was Al-Ghazali, who succeeded in both theory and practice in silencing philosophy and instead establishing the science of Kalam, and making it official in the Muslim religious schools and universities.

Islamic philosophy, broadly speaking, began in the third (ninth) century after a large number of Greek philosophical texts, especially Aristotle and Plato's, had been translated into Arabic. Both these philosophers had a decisive influence in shaping the rational framework of Islamic philosophical thought. Even Al-Ghazali utilized the Idealism of Plato and Neo-Platonism in constructing his anti-philosophical theology. But the Muslim philosophers, being interested in finding answers to the contradictions of Islamic civilization, were attracted towards Aristotle's rationalism and Plato's political philosophy. Their main concern was to bring about a sort of reconciliation between Revelation and Reason or Islam and Greek philosophy. For example, al-Farabi sought to harmonize the Platonic conception of philosopher-king and divine Law, Sharia.

His attempt had a great influence on the well-known Andalusian philosopher Ibn Rushd (Averroes), the last representative of Greek philosophy in the Islamic world before Ibn Khaldun, who became known in the West as the Commentator of Aristotle.

Ibn-Rushd wrote *tahafut-al tahafut*, the Incoherence of Incoherence, in response to Al-Ghazali's Incoherence of Philosophers. He also wrote the Harmony between Philosophy and History, in which he tried to harmonize

Reason and Revelation by establishing them as two independent modes of reaching the truth.

Ibn Khaldun adapted this distinction, regarding man responsible for the realisation of his life without any divine intervention. Proceeding from his own political experiences, he could envisage all the aspects of human life in terms of the materiality of man's political struggle.

He found no contradiction between this view and the basic Quranic principles, which, if rightly interpreted, call for rationality, wisdom and justice. In fact, he provides a religious setting for his philosophical and sociological arguments, relying on Quranic verses to vindicate his materialist interpretation of the world. But the Quran gives principles only without analysing, explaining or briefing them. It was philosophy, which had to undertake this task. Hence, his recourse to the rational arguments of Greek philosophy. Therefore, the question of harmonizing religion and philosophy was not, for Ibn Khaldun, a sheer tactical procedure; it was a strategic necessity for the purpose of serving the truth which his book Al-Muqaddima tries to establish.

Chapter Two

CONSTRUCTING A SCIENCE OF HISTORY

1.1 Foreword

In his famous description of Ibn Khaldun's Al-Muqaddima Arnold Toynbee writes: "Ibn Khaldun has conceived and formulated a philosophy of history which is undoubtedly the greatest work of its kind that has ever yet been produced by any mind in any time or place."

While the greatness of this work has been taken for granted, the articulation of Ibn Khaldun's philosophy in different aspects and arguments of Ibn Khaldun's thought has been subject to different interpretations and view-points. The studies of Ibn Khaldun's work have generally been conducted in terms of its appropriation by one or another of academic or ideological disciplinary discourses. In other words, they have been generally been conducted in terms of a bourgeois Euro-centric conception of history and knowledge. Ibn Khaldun has not been free from being appropriated by Orientalism, i.e., Western bourgeois interpretations linked with imperialist ideology. Yves Lacoste, for example, gives the following interpretation:

> "But Ibn Khaldun was the only one to produce, several hundred years before the arrival of the Europeans, such a methodical description of the successive crises that arose; he alone looked for the causes of stagnation in the internal structures of the society in which he lived rather than in some divinely ordained plan or in external causes. He found no solution or remedy simply because none was to exist for several hundred years to come: those stagnant and restrictive societies could only be destroyed by the action of a force emanating from a foreign and <u>qualitatively different society</u>."

It is not the aim of this chapter to discuss or repudiate such interpretations. What I would like to do is simply to allow the text, Al-Muqaddima, to speak for itself. I shall confine my analysis to the investigation of the modality of Ibn Khaldun's <u>theoretical practice</u> without the understanding of which, I think, it is not possible to reconstruct Ibn Khaldun's great enterprise as the first scientific theory of history. The starting-point of this chapter is the belief that any kind of knowledge is produced in the context of history and society. But any epoch-making theoretical practice such as Ibn Khaldun's cannot be but the result of an epistemological break with traditional knowledge and mode of thinking. As it stands, this paper serves as an introduction to a broader and comprehensive study of the various dimensions of Ibn Khaldun's thought taken as aspects of one unified scientific philosophical conception of history.

1.2 The Threshold

A most striking characteristic of al-Muqaddima (1) is its self-consciousness. As a theory of history, it is conscious of its problematic, which itself is constituted by means of theoretical-rational practise. Ibn Khaldun systematically expounds his own conception of the world through his critical elaboration of a methodology of history triggered by a new insight into the nature of historical events. But this novel insight was not the product of an abstract desire for intellectualism and innovation. It was made possible by a rational response to the epistemological challenge presented by the spirit of his time and his own deep-rooted political and intellectual involvement in its events.

The fourteenth century in which Ibn Khaldun lived and wrote, witnessed the widening of the gap between the dynamics of history on the one hand and its theological interpretation, on the other. This was an idealistic interpretation based on the religious world view that historical events are, in fact, supra-historical: unfoldings of the divine will, inscriptions of the Almighty's justice and wisdom. But such an interpretation had not only failed to account for the decline and decay of Islamic civilization especially in North Africa where Ibn Khaldun lived but, retrospectively, it was also contradicted by the fact that even the ideal model of God's state on the earth, the Islamic caliphate itself, was also vulnerable to internal conflict and structural decay: a phenomenon which required a satisfactory explanation. But, to Ibn Khaldun, it was the designation of the problem itself which was paramount rather than superseding the traditional interpretations with new speculative ones. The question had to be formulated a new before their answer could be sought. Hence, the theoretical nature of his enterprise.

Radical theoretical intervention in the realm of traditional thinking cannot but mark a double-edged epistemological rupture exposing the theoretical and historical impotence of the conservative thought, and creating scientific theoretical conditions for enabling the revolutionary breakthrough of new ideas and vision. Ibn Khaldun was aware of this position. His new science was not to be merely a new method of writing history, but a new methodology; a new conception of the world marked by a radical break with all traditional Islamic sciences -all of which were either originated in and informed by the Quran and Sunna (Mohammad's explanations of the Quranic text and his mode of life) or referred by analogy to the laws that were believed to be incarnated in Quran words and Tradition, combining all forms of knowledge:

> "All scientific knowledge, says Ibn Khaldun, deals with ideas the mind and imagination; this applies to the religious sciences in which research in mostly concerned with words and the substance of which is the laws derived from the

Quran, the Sunna and language used in them that leads to (the formulation of) these laws." (vol. 3 pp. 315-316)

Thus all Islamic sciences were by definition linguistic-spiritual sciences; for they were either directly derived from Quranic word, law or had an analogical affinity with them that could be deciphered by a rational gaze, and established by the consensus of Muslim 'ulamas'. They were considered noble sciences and the noblest of them was the nearest to the creator, the science of the unity of God, as al-Ghazali calls it (3). On the other hand, those forms of knowledge which mind and imagination failed to trace their affinity to Quranic laws were labelled as "the sciences of sorcery and talismans", considered illegitimate and deprived of the right of existence. (vol. 3. pp. I 56-i70) Even physics, as a science dealing with physical bodies, things as such, without designating them as sings of the divine power, was considered hostile and irrelevant. For things, like word and ideas, were conceived to signify nothing but power and essence.

> "The power combining everything without any particularization is divine power. It is the power distributed over all existing things, whether they are universals or particulars, combining and comprising them in every aspect, with regard to appearance and hid-den ness and with regard to form and matter. Every thing is one. One-ness is identical with the divine essence." (Vol. 3 pp 89-90)

This religious view, more or less, constitutes what we may call, using Foucault's terminology, 'the episteme' that had dominated Islamic thought (theology, Sufism and Jurisprudence), until the last quarter of the fourteenth century when Ibn Khaldun's solitary intervention established a major theoretical break. Although Muslim scholars had been familiarized with Greek philosophy since the eighth century and this had aroused serious theoretical debates about the oneness of God, anthropomorphism, the status of the Quran...etc, the direction which these debates had eventually taken was towards the reassertion and consolidation of the authority of the Islamic speculative theology, Kalam, which, itself, had emerged as a theoretical science to defend the articles of faith against the rationalist challenge of philosophers who were regarded as enemies of faith because, as Ibn Khaldun tells us "in most respects there is a relationship between the opinion of the innovators and the opinion of the philosophers." (vol. 3 p. 52)

However in the process of combating philosophy Islamic theology itself, as we shall see later, was largely rationalized. Having the same problem as that of philosophy, it allowed itself to draw freely on philosophical methods of argument without jeopardizing its traditional dogmas, establishing its subject as " how the articles of faith which the religious law had laid down as correct, can be proven with the help of logical argument. In other words, logical arguments were subordinated to the authoritarianism of the traditional dogmas which defined the acceptable boundaries of both theoretical and practical knowledge. Any form of intellectual dissent was to be dubbed as heretical and hence suppressed and silenced. By the time of Ibn Khaldun theology itself, having duly systematized the Islamic episteme, and having established the authority of the Islamic Law, was no longer necessary.

> "The science of speculative theology is not something that is necessary to the contemporary student. Heretic and innovation have been destroyed. The orthodox religious leaders have given us protection against heretics and innovators in their systematic works and treatment."(vol. 3. p. 56)

But this victory of orthodox theology was not applauded by history. For it did not signify a parallel success of Islamic civilization which was, on the contrary, declining and decaying everywhere. Theology could offer no rational explanation. It was in this historical conjuncture that Ibn Khaldun felt he had to grasp the moment of genesis of a new science, the science of history. For speculative theology had not only excluded history from its arguments, but it had also relegated Islamic historiography, being a mundane discipline, into an appendage of Tradition, a technique for verifying the chain of the transmitters of Tradition, a genealogical record of Caliphs, or a mere mechanism of reporting factual events and accumulation of empirical data.

Thus Islamic historiography by the time of Ibn Khaldun, despite some great achievements in terms of historical knowledge, had emerged as a gigantic accumulative corpus of misinformation, myth and uncritical reports and descriptions of events, countries and races: Accumulation for accumulation's sake with no bearing on the rational interpretation of historical process. In short, historiography as a discipline was ripe for a qualitative leap. The task that Ibn Khaldun found himself confronted with was to establish historiography as a science: to demarcate its domain, designate its nature and define its object of knowledge. At this point, it is important to stress the fact that while Ibn Khaldun, as we shall see later, found the theoretical conditions of the possibility of this aspired science in philosophy, particularly in Aristotle's science of logic, what triggered his point of departure from traditional thought was his political awareness (as an actor not just an interested spectator in the turbulent events of his time) of the phenomenon of change as an area overlooked by traditional historians who "disregarded the change in conditions and in the customs of the nations and races that the passing of time, has brought about. "(vol. I p.9) This awareness of the dynamics of time, its function of distancing the dominating episteme from concrete historical situation, provided Ibn Khaldun with an empirical space in which he could locate an independent science of history. But this science had to obtain the theoretical conditions of its possibility which could be found nowhere but in philosophy. Ibn Khaldun's acute awareness of the spirit of his age and his great intellectual insight and concern about the fate of human civilization in the historical conjuncture of the fourteenth century are strongly reflected in the following passage in which he describes the way he viewed the great changes of his time:

> "When there is a great change of conditions, it is as if the entire creation had changed and the whole world had been altered, as if it were a new and repeated creation, as world brought into existence anew. Therefore, there is a need at this time that someone should systematically set down the situation of the world among all regions and races…" (vol. I p. 63)

This means that it is the seriousness of the historical conjuncture which calls for a universal history. But to Ibn Khaldun this task was to be far greater than "someone's merely setting down the situation of the world." It involved first of all the necessity of obtaining a new vision of the changed and changing situation, and a new method of approaching history. For the passing of time had made the dominant traditional concepts and modes of thinking completely futile. The object of historical concern itself had changed. Historical significance was no more focused on leaders, rulers and personalities. He writes:

> "The problem now was which nations could stand up and which were too weak to do so." (ibid. P. 63)

In other words, what were at stake now were real issues of life and destiny; the very survival of nations and groups in the context of power struggle and national hegemony. Having found the methods and approaches of Islamic historiography too erroneous, irrational and unscientific to be of any help in carrying out his project, Ibn Khaldun embarked upon constructing his own methodology by brilliantly harmonizing both his philosophical and historical insights, synthesizing a new science, the science of history. Here, we have this striking aspect of theoretical radicalism in his approach; the cohabitation of philosophy and history. "History…. is firmly rooted in philosophy. It deserves to be accounted a branch of philosophy." (vol. I. p. 6)

1.3 Philosophy and religion

Philosophically, Ibn Khaldun was well-equipped to invest the positivist space of his would-be since. But this intellectual adequacy was first of all to be reconciled with the predominant ethos of his Islamic milieu which identified philosophy as an ominous recalcitrant alien whose passport to the territory of the established Islamic cultural could be nothing less than the proviso of its total submission to the authority of theology. An attempt at reconciling theology and philosophy on the basis of defining them as tow independent modes of reading truth had already been made by Ibn-Rushd (Averroes), the last representative of Greek philosophy in the Islamic world. But this project had been dismantled by al-Ghazali and

Ibn Rushd's books in the Islamic east had been destroyed. However, as we have mentioned before, speculative theology itself had accommodated logic as the method of argument although Muslim theologians tried to distinguish it form philosophy proper and emphasize its values as a pure methodological discipline.

> "They made a distinction between it and the philosophical sciences in that logic was merely a norm and yardstick for argument and served to probe the argument of the (philosophical sciences) as well as (those of) all other (disciplines)". (vol. 3. p 51)

What entailed the theologian's recourse to logic was the fact that theology had the same problematic as that of philosophy and, therefore, was entrapped in the same epistemological domain. They

> "deduced the existence and attributes of the Creator from the existing things and their conditions. As a rule, this was their line of argument. The physical bodies from part of the existing things, and they are subject of the philosophical study of physics" (Ibid. p. 52)

If we know that logic in its systematized Aristotelian form had, according to Ibn Khaldun, occupied "its proper place as the first philosophical discipline and the introduction to philosophy", (vol. 3. p. 39) we can understand to what extent speculative theology approximated a philosophical status. But what suppressed the philosophical (rational) function of logic was theology's dogmatism, its total adherence to the articles of faith. In other word, logic was not resorted to for the purpose of, let's say, discovering truth, but to verify pre-established truths and defend them against rational challenges. This caused crucial deviation from the tendency of philosophical study.

> "The philosophers study bodies in so far as they move or are stationary. The theologians, on the other hand, study them in so far as they serve as an argument for the Maker. In the same way philosophical study of metaphysics studies

existence as such and what it requires for its essence. The theological study (of metaphysics) on the other hand, is concerned with the existentia, in so far as they serve an argument for Him who creates existence." (vol. 3. pp. 52-53)

Theological sciences tend to studying physical bodies as sings of their creator. Given the similarity of subject and method, philosophy was eventually entrapped in the problematic of theology, usurped and deprived of its distinctive identity. Ibn Khaldun remarks:

"Recent speculative theologians, then, confused the problems of theology with those of philosophy, because the investigations of theology and philosophy go in the same direction, and the subject and problems of theology are similar to the subject and problems of metaphysics... thus, in a way came to be one and the same discipline." (vol. 3. p. i53)

The initial task that confronted Ibn Khaldun, then, was to emancipate logic as a rational method of research from its theological and metaphysical problematic. And this could be done not only by separating theology and logic as two distinct and independent modes of knowledge, but also by delimiting the worlds or domains of their activity. This separation, however, is not, for Ibn Khaldun, just a tactical measure aimed at neutralising the influence of theology in the question of historical process. It is, in fact, a rational and moral necessity which serves to locate faith in those epistemic spaces which man's faculty of reason cannot fill in. Ibn Khaldun agrees with al-Ghazali's sceptic attitude that man's insistence on grasping the truth of such questions as the identity of God is irrational because they are beyond human ability of thinking. They are, therefore to be accepted as matters of faith. That is we must accept the traditional prescription on the unknowability of such questions.

"Muhammad did not inform us about the real being of this worshipped creator, because it something too difficult

> for our perception and above our level. He made it our first obligation to believe that he in his essence cannot be compared with created being". (vol. 3. p. 44, p. 154)

Therefore, once in our rational tracing of the series of causality we reach the causer of causes, Him who brings them into existence, we must stop. To pursue further and desire to query His essence is a sheer vanity. Even in nature while causality itself is a phenomenon that can be experienced the action of causality itself, as essence, is unknowable. It can be known as relationship only.

> "The way in which the causes exercise their influence upon the majority of the caused in unknown. They are only known through customary (experience) or through conclusions which attest (the existence) of an apparent causal relationship. What the influence really is and how it takes place is not known." (vol. 3. p. 36)

This, as it will be clear later, does not mean that Ibn Khaldun holds a nominalist position. It simply means that the 'absolute' truth of causality is no more than the 'relative' truth as it manifests itself in causal 'relationships'. Man, Ibn Khaldun thinks, has a corporal and a spiritual composition, his spirituality being mixed with his material being. And it is his spirit, his mental capacity which is capable of perceiving the outside world. But it can do that through man's corporal part; the intermediary of the organs of the body such as the senses and the brain. However, Ibn Khaldun distinguishes another level of perception which he calls 'spiritual perception' which mind can perceive 'through its own essence' without any corporal mediation. But this ability of mind is restricted to prophetic and mystic visions which can penetrate the veil of material existence and attain the perception of spiritual essence (pure intellection). The cognizance of the material world, however, is possible only through senses and brain.

Ibn Khaldun located his epistemological strategy in this differentiation between the spiritual and the material. Revelation and speculative theology are concerned with supernatural and moral questions because they are equipped to do this. But mind, i.e., rational discourse, must be devoted to the affairs of our world. Revelation, Muhammad's perception, is wider and more comprehensive than that of ordinary human perceptions, but

> "This does not speak against intellectual and intellectual perception. The intellect, indeed, is a correct scale. Its indications are completely certain and in no way wrong. However, the intellect should not be used to weight such matters as the oneness of God, the other world, the truth of prophecy, the real character of the divine attribute, or anything else that lies beyond the level of the intellect. This would mean to desire the impossible. There is a limit at which the intellect must stop. It cannot go beyond its own level… this shows that those who give the intellect preference over (traditional) information in such matters are wrong, deficient in understanding and faulty in reasoning." (Ibid. p. 38)

The argument is clear. Revelation, the Quranic discourse, by virtue of its divine capacity to surpass man's mental limitation, is superior to mind. This should be admitted. And mind should not aspire to the impossible to divulge what it cannot. But, and this is the other side of the argument, this, at the same time, should release mind, this correct scale, to exercise its activity in the realm of man's material existence. Mind should not be suppressed and silenced by tradition and its dogmas. What Ibn Khaldun has achieved out of this compromise is distancing mind, and consequently logic, from the problematic of theology and metaphysics. He has restored to reason its independence and enabled it to operate in those areas of historical and civilizational problems which the fourteenth century had highlightened. Ibn Khaldun's secularization of the material world, the world of man, goes so far that he strongly rejects the argument that prophecy is a logical necessity. Man, he argues, can arrange his affairs and organize society without any divine intervention. This is clear from the history of many nations who have never had divine books but managed to build civilization.

"The philosophers are wrong when they assume that prophecy exists by necessity. The existence of prophecy is not required by logic. Its necessary character is indicated by the religious law." (vol. I. p. 7. Also p. 390)

Thus Ibn Khaldun emphasises that the necessity of prophecy is only a moral obligation indicated by religious law and not a logical necessity vindicated by reason or by the realities of human life. In short, history is the function of man alone: his needs, his thinking and his action, in the context of his material existence.

1.4 Towards a scientific theory of knowledge

Having been released from its theological and metaphysical mesh, mind is enabled now to invest its activity in such empirical realms as history and civilization. But the function of mind, however, is not given and arbitrary. In order to be able to acquire desired 'scientific' knowledge in any domain, mind should be aware of its own practise, i.e. of the rules and laws of its activity. To Ibn Khaldun at least, the science of logic in its systematized Aristotelian form as "the first philosophical discipline and the introduction to philosophy" represented this condition of mind's self-awareness which, translated into a system would mean nothing but a theory of knowledge applicable to all spheres of human existence. Before entering into details of such a theory, let us consider his definition of Aristotle's science of logic and its implications for his scientific project of historical knowledge.

"Logic studies analogical reasoning from the point of view of the desired (information) it is expected to yield. It studies what the premises (of the desired information) ought to be, as seen in this light, and to which kind a certain or hypothetical knowledge the (desired information) belongs. Logic studies analogical reasoning not with some particular object in mind but exclusively with regard to the way in which it is produced." (vol. 3. p. 140)

Projecting the constituents of this definition into a theoretical framework of a proposed science of history we will have the following requirements:

- To define the desired information (which is historical knowledge).
- A rational scrutiny of the theoretical conditions of its production. This involves a critical investigation of the nature of the traditional historical information.
- To formulate the premises (principles) of the new science.
- To define its domain (theoretically it belongs to philosophy).
- To define the object of the new science.

This final element is of extraordinary significance. It is the determining step in departing from logic as a mere method concerned with the way knowledge, any knowledge, is capable of justifying itself rationally, and using it instead as a theoretical ground for a new empirical science. On the other hand, it is the constitution of an independent peculiar object which makes possible the formulation of a new problematic of the theory of history and hence establishing it as a scientific theory. Let us start with the question of 'premises': no method is possible without first establishing its principles. In fact, arguments of any theory are to a large extent determined by the principles and assumptions from which they ensue. The initial question to be reconstructed, therefore, concerns the nature of principles, i.e. of philosophy itself. This inevitably leads to the formulation of the question as that of relationship between matter and thought, or experience and knowledge.

Fortunately, Ibn Khaldun was too well-schooled in Islamic tradition, and familiar with its epistemic position to be unaware of the risk of falling into the pitfalls of dogmatism represented by the then two dominant trends of Islamic thought, speculative theology and Sufism. It did not suffice for Ibn Khaldun to divorce logic from its theological-metaphysical problematic. He had to underpin his theoretical rapture with new epistemological elaborations that would preclude the intervention of the idealist negativism of traditional thought which tended to the canonization of 'premises'. Ibn Khaldun's option for elaborating a materialist conception of the world was, as we shall see, a logical outcome of his critical rejection of the epistemological positions of both theological dogmatism and Sufism. He rejected the first because "rational arguments were used only after the correctness of the articles of faith, as they had been received and believed in by the early Muslims and which had been stipulated by traditional evidence". (vol. 3. p. 154). In other words, the theology's rational system was based upon methods of proof which lead to conclusions identical with its dogmatic principles. This, according to Ibn Khaldun, reduced rational argument to 'formal analogical reasoning' as "the universal and the essential, for speculative theologians," is merely a mental concept having no correspondence outside (the mind) (Ibid). Also, Ibn Khaldun rejects the Sufist conception of the world, describing it as erroneous, irrational and unscientific:

> "The Sufi perceptions are the one that are least scientific. The Sufis claim intuitive experience in connection with their perception and shun (rational) evidence. But intuitive experience is far removed from scientific perceptions and ways and things that go with them". (vol. 3. p. 155)

The Sufis had a subjective idealist vision of the world based on what Ibn Khaldun describes as one's 'superficial impression' that "the whole of existence is comprised of his perceptions". (vol. 3. p. 37). Ultimately, this vision leads to the identification of the world with 'ego': that the world's variation and particularization exist only in man's faculty of differentiation.

> "If there were no perceptions to create distinctions there would be no particularization, but just one perception, namely the 'I' and nothing else". (vol. 3. p. 91)

But perception for Sufists did not signify a medium or a way of acquiring knowledge. It was a pre-given imaginative faculty, the power of intuition. So, as Ibn Khaldun explains it, "when they say imaginary they do not mean 'imaginary' as part (in the sequence) of human perception" (Ibid). Between the lines of above quotation, we can glean how Ibn Khaldun envisages a theoretical alternative; a scientific theory of perception as a sequence comprising parts; as process. And in his detailed critique of both theological and Sufis idealisms, he elaborates some important theses towards a materialist conception of the world:

1. That existence cannot be identified with one's perceptions because the latter are relative and imperfect and cannot as such be relied on as correct measures of knowing the outside world:

"A deaf person feels that the whole of existence is comprised in the perceptions of his four senses and his intellect. The whole group of audible things constitutes no part of existence for him. The same applies to a blind person...etc" (vol. 3. p. 37)

1. On the other hand the world of existence is too vast for man's knowledge to encompass it in its totality. In particular, mind cannot know the supernatural world.
2. The world exists independently and outside man's perceptions:

"We know for certain that a country which we have quitted on our travels or to which we are travelling exist despite the fact that we do not see it any more. We also have definite knowledge of the existence of heaven and of the stars, and of all other things that are remote from us." (vol. 3. p. 91)

The world exists objectively, independently of man's experiencing it. It is knowable and man is able to know it. But how does this act of knowing occur? The crucial point now is the way Ibn Khaldun seeks to fill in the epistemic space between the subject (mind) and the object, the world of existence, as he calls it.

Does Ibn Khaldun approach the world as a subject of contemplation, or as an object of material, perceptive, practical activity of man? The decisive step in this respect is his rejection of the idea of an absolute pre-constituted conscious subject or cognitive faculty. Albeit he accepts the definition of thinking as 'innate, God-given ability', he makes it clear that man is not a knowing thinking subject as such. Man is 'primarily matter', 'essentially ignorant' and, in reality, simply an animal. (vol. 2. pp.

424-426). His humanity is not an ontological property, but an unrealized potential which can only be materialized historically through his practical involvement in living as a domain of necessity. The completion of man's humanity can be approached theoretically as the evolutionary process of his thinking ability:

> "God distinguished man from all other animals by an ability to think which he made the beginning of human perfection and the end of man's noble superiority over existent things". (vol. 2. p. 411)

The process of thinking is then, the process of man's self-humanization and, at the same time, of establishing his superiority over other beings. But this process does not occur in mind or spirit. It is a completely materially-conditioned process. Man has not inherited knowledge as such from God; but God has made him able to acquire knowledge by giving him, as the Quran states, 'hearing, vision and hearts', i.e., the organs of sensation and thinking. On the other hand, knowledge is possible only because the world upon which man's perceptive power acts is also material, and it is perceptible because of its materiality, its solid construction and causal nexuses.

> "The world with all created things it has a certain order and solid construction. It shows nexuses between causes and things caused, combination of some parts of creation with others, and transformation of some existent things into others, in a pattern that is both remarkable and endless." (vol. I. p. 194)

The important core of this concept is its interpretation of the world both as a relationship (causal nexuses and structural combinations) and as a process (patterned transformations). These two aspects cannot be separated. Processing takes place by virtue of the fact that things are interconnected. As a rule, processing or becoming takes an ascending order. Thus the world of creation started out from the mineral and gradually progressed to plants, such as herbs and seedless plants. The last stage of plants, such as vines and palms is connected with the first stage of animals such as snail and shellfish which have only the power stage of animals, such as vines and palms is connected with the first stage of animals such as snails and shellfish which have only the power of touch. And finally 'in a gradual process of creation' the last stage of animal world, i.e. monkeys, leads to man who owns an innate potentiality to think and reflect. This process of becoming is possible because of the interconnectedness and interpenetration of the material elements of creation.

Ibn Khaldun explains:

> "The word 'connection' with regard to this created thing, means that last stage of each group is fully prepared to become the first stage of the next group." (vol. 1. p. 195)

The evolutionary process of the world is a clear articulation of the interconnected nexuses and combination of its parts and elements.

Man himself, as differentiated from other beings by his power of perception and thinking, is the highest from of matter produced by this process. And what connects the possibility of man as a perceiving subject and the possibility of the material world as an intelligible order is the law of motion. Perception is possible only because the world is arranged in layers which are interconnected, in a shape which the senses are able to perceive only through the existence of motions! (vol. 1 p. 195). Motion, to Ibn Khaldun, is what constitutes the phenomenon of spirituality and he conceives it as "soul". This spiritual phenomenon represents both the capability of matter i.e. ., the objective world of being perceived and of the highly developed "human" matter, the organs of sensation, and brain, of perceiving its shape and order. For motion/ spirituality is the property of both of them (vol I p. 197) Eye, for example, is a corporal organ but" seeing" is its spiritual property. The same thing can be said about ears and hearing, tongue and talking, legs and walking, and especially brain and the whole complex process of thinking. This property of matter establishes a common ground for the unity of the universal process of matter in both its physical and spiritual forms. In other words, the unity of the laws of matter and consciousness, for perception also, like the material processes of the world, processes in an ascending gradation initiated by man's being and acting in the world. In fact, man's rational potentiality of differentiation is, to Ibn Khaldun, essentially linked with his being in the world as a political as well as rational agent. As man is God's representative on the earth, "God enabled them (human beings) to arrange for (their activities) under political aspects and according to philosophical norms". (vol. 2 p. 418)

But his political tendency, his need for action in a pre-conceived manner entailed by his biological status as a weak animal and hence his vital need for social organisation, is primary and determinant. Therefore, the laws of human knowledge are, at the same time, the laws of his social and civilization process. But this, however, does not mean the identification and inseparability of these two processes. Mind is capable of establishing its own independent realm. However, Ibn Khaldun distinguishes there levels of mind's epistemological development:

1. Discerning intellect. This is the natural dimension of mind i.e., the function of senses in their contact with the world of things. It produces perceptions which are common among all living beings, but for man, these perceptions are elementary and pragmatic. They form a basis for intentional actions and lead to a higher form of knowledge. (vol. 2 pp. 4i2-413)
2. Experimental intellect. This level represents the social dimension of mind. That is to say, it is the product of man's politicality: his vital need to enter into mutual relationships with his fellow men. It enhances man's ability to think about his existential state as well as the outside world. Man learns from his experiences and acquires apperceptions. He can induce from empirical events proper concepts and norms of behaviour. But in this stage, man does not need to induce all lessons, habits and concepts from everyday life. He can receive them ready-made from former generations. This constitutes an extra-empirical source of knowledge which is patterned as tradition and diffused in society through co-existence and instruction. However, the main teacher of man remains life itself. He who is not educated by his parents, will be educated by time".(vol. 2 p. 413)
3. Speculative intellect. This is the highest level of man's thinking activity developed from the former two levels. It represents what

we may call the philosophical dimension of mind. i.e., its ability to produce hypothetical knowledge: to grasp existence as it is by abstracting it from the conditions of its necessity by means of rational devices such as analysis, synthesis, deduction and analogy. In so doing, man transfers existence into an abstract reality. In other words, existence is now man's verbal image and mental concept of it. This level signifies the perfection of man's ability to think and his gaining control over the outside world while still possessing potentiality to transfer into a further level: the level of angels or total spirituality. But this is an esoteric mission and only prophets by virtue of their natural divine disposition and some Sufis, through certain somato-spiritual exercises, can achieve.

According to the above schema, the identity of knowledge is decided by the development of man's cognitive capacity, in the context of his being and acting in the world, in an ascending order: natural, social (historical) and metaphysical (philosophical). What decisively differentiates man from nature and animal world is his ability to use the law of motion/his perceptive power consciously and intentionally and thus not to be stuck in a certain uniliniar and, deterministic mode of development, but to have capacity to move "upwards and downwards" I. e., between spiritual and physical world according to the conditions of his living and his material and spiritual needs. (vol. 1 p. 196 and pp. 434-435) Thus man, and his society, is liable to both evolution and devolution: to progress towards the world of angels, or degenerate into, the world of beasts. As we can notice, Ibn Khaldun's theory of knowledge allows the establishment of knowledge or thought as an ultimately independent mode of existence which itself can become a major part of human reality, reproduce itself in language, and exercise a significant influence on man's Gnostic mode of being. Here we face the danger of traditionalism which stultifies man's rational ability and blinds him to the reality of his historical existence: also the danger of rational dogmatism: one's fantasy that his mental images can represent concrete reality. In this context, the question of truth becomes extremely opaque and enigmatic, unless we obtain a correct criteriology of it. But this criteriology cannot be located merely within the epistemological zone itself. It must be based on the accountability of any hypothesis to the material objects and conditions for which it stands as their alleged truth, but, taken as mere verbal generalization, cannot conform to. On this argument Ibn Khaldun bases his refutation of metaphysics. (vol. 3 pp. 246-258). By means of analytical reasoning, mind can reduce the complex materiality of existence into universals I.e., mental concepts that are simple (vol. 3 p. 138). But these concepts must not be absolute. What we must always emphasize is the contingency of hypothetical knowledge on perception as the primary and actual medium of knowing reality, without detracting from the scientific significance of rational abstraction.

"In fact (apperception) ultimately reverts to perception because the only use of having (perception) is to (achieve) knowledge of the realities of things, which is the required goal of appreciative knowledge." (vol. 3 pp. 138-139)

It follows that the theoretical premises of any scientific project must remain firmly rooted in the reality of things that constitute the object of a given science. In short, the truth of knowledge should be decided by proceeding from the concrete to the abstract and back to the concrete again. This procedure is necessary to preclude the mutation of theoretical premises into metaphysical dogmas.

1.1 Towards a scientific theory of history

This scientific vision of the nature of truth stood in total opposition to both theological dogmatism and Sufism, both of which subordinated truth to supra-historical sources and thus divorced discourse from any empirical value. This metaphysical mode of thinking had in particular far-reaching repercussions for historical knowledge. It deprived historiography of critical insight and riddled it with errors, contradictions and gaps:

> "Historians, Quran commentators and leading transmitters have committed frequent errors in the stories and events they reported. They accepted them in the plain transited form, without regard for its value. They did not check them with the principles underlying such historical situations, nor did they compare them

> with similar materials. Also they did not probe (more deeply) with the yardstick of philosophy, with the help of knowledge of nature of things, or with the help of speculation and historical insight. Therefore, they strayed from the truth and found themselves lost in the desert of baseless assumptions and errors." (vol.1)

Therefore of the argument in a general sense is that it is the lack of a scientific method of approaching historical information that makes the historian lost in the desert of baseless assumptions and errors. And the purport of al-Muqaddima is to construct such a method in order to rid historical discourse of its illusory shell and grasp what Ibn Khaldun calls "the inner meaning of history" which

> "Involves speculation and an attempt to get at truth, subtle explanation of the causes and origins of the existent things, and deep knowledge of the how and why of events." (vol. 1 p. 6)

The question of the criteriology of truth as Ibn Khaldun construes it in the above two quotations involves two crucial interdependent levels of scrutiny which correspond to the epistemological nature of his enterprise as a unification of both philosophical and historical insights, and his conception of man as both a political and philosophical being.

- First: the relation of truth to the theoretical conditions of its possibility. That is, to probe the epistemological nature of error.
- Second: the theory's relation to the world, to the "why and how" of things i.e., the empirical conditions of its truth.

Traditional historiography was hollowed at both levels: at the theoretical level because of the lack of any scientific sense of methodology, and at the empirical level because of the lack of historical insight. Thus, when a great Muslim historian like al-Masudi reports the army of Israelites in the time of Moses as numbering 600,000 or more, he does so without conducting any rational investigation of the conditions of possibility of such a claim which, as Ibn Khaldun argues can be refuted on the basis of many logical and historical grounds (vol. 1 pp. 16-21). But Muslim historians were satisfied with registering such exaggerated figures, motivated by a common desire for sensualism. (p.20).

Another example of these typical errors is al-Masudi's story of "an alleged copper city.. In the desert of Silmash which Musa Ibn Nusayr crossed on his raid against Maghreb...?" Is the existence of a copper city possible? The question of possibility, according to Ibn Khaldun's criteriology, has two levels: within the discourse as reported information signifying a historical situation in a given observable spatial setting. This can be scrutinized by way of comparing information. In this case the story proves to be absurd because "the desert of Silmash has been crossed by travellers and guides. They have not come across any information about such a city". But science is more than explaining the truth by referring to what is actual. It also establishes unobservable conditions that explain the observable ones and enable us to judge their possible state of affairs. science dose this by means of external criteria, external but rational and scientific, i.e., capable of being verified by empirical means. From this standpoint we find also that:

> "The details of copper city are absurd (if compared with) the customary state of affairs. they contradict natural facts that apply to the building and planning of cities. Metal exists at best in quantities sufficient for utensils and furnishings. It is really absurd and unlikely that there would be enough to cover a city with it."(vol. 1 p. 76)

Thus, it is only by means of our acquiring a rational (philosophical) insight into the nature of events that we can distinguish truth from falsehood and phenomenal mystifications:

> "Every event (or phenomena), whether (it come into being in connection with some) essence or (as the result of an) action, must inevitably possess a nature peculiar to its essence as well as to the accidental conditions that may

> attach themselves to it. If the student knows the nature of events and its circumstances and requirements in the world of existence, it will help him to distinguish truth from untruth in investigating the historical information critically." (vol. 1)

Again the two basic levels of an event's or a phenomenon's mode of existence are emphasized that

1. an event possess a nature peculiar to its essence i.e., its own specificity, its own mode of occurrence, and
2. this specificity is not independently self-constitutive but it is related to its circumstances and requirements in the world of existence.

It makes no difference whether this relationship is immediate and observable in the spatial dimension of the phenomenon or whether it is constituted by science through man's rational grasp of the logic of the relationship of things in the world. What characterizes this Khaldunic understanding of historical event is its freedom from idealistic elemi nets. What has value now is the event itself, its mode of existence and all possible conditions of its articulation. Even super structural (ideological) elements (such as religion) can operate historically only by their becoming a part of the attached conditions of the event, i.e., by their interaction with its specificity. (See, for example, vol. 1 p. 418).

Given this theoretical clarity about the modality of historical events, what history lacks to become a science is the designation of its own specific object and formulation of its own problematic. As we have seen, Ibn Khaldun has rejected the idea of history as a ruler-centred narrative, as a fictional space for the outlet of frustrated desires (vol. 1 p. 40), as a domain for fabricating random statements and reporting fables and absurd tales. And, although he appreciates the empirical value and originality of the works of some great historians such as al-Masudi and al-Bakri, he is equally critical of their failure to elaborate a rational interpretation of historical event, especially the phenomenon of the decay of human civilization. History, to be correctly understood, should be freed from all that is irrelevant to the understanding of historical act in its true natural and rational manifestation. Then we can see it as nothing but the function of man in his pursuance of bettering the conditions of his living. As man is political by nature, as soon as a group of human being enter into mutual co-operation to fulfil their primary needs of survival and form some kind of social organization, umran (urbanisation or civilization) comes into being. Therefore, civilization is identical with social organization and it is the cognizance of their nature which "makes critical investigation of them possible". (vol. 1 p.78)

In other words, social organization(human civilization) is history's own peculiar object and only after recognizing this we can talk of history as an independent science (p. 77), the problematic of which is constituted by the relation of its peculiar object to, and its function in, the surrounding world. That is, its problematic manifests itself in "explaining the conditions that attach themselves to the essence of civilization one after another" (p.76). This gives us a normative criteriology for distinguishing truth from falsehood in historical information. But this normative method does not emanate from any pre-conceived norms. It is based on the information's own ground of possibility or absurdity:

> "To investigate human social organization this is identical with civilization. We must distinguish the conditions that attach themselves to the essence of civilization as required by its very nature: the things that are accidental (to civilization) and cannot be counted on: and the things that can possibly attach themselves to it." (p.77)

He goes on further to demarcate the domain of his science and distinguish it from Aristotle's logical disciplines and his Politics. He rightly asserts that it is his novel "extraordinary" object: social organization, which gives his science its originality and radicalism. True, Greeks, Persians and Arabs had more or less touched on this subject. But they had done this only casually and none had ever tried to make it an object of a critical scientific investigation. It was Ibn Khaldun who, for the first time in the history of human thought, achieved this epoch-making task. And he achieved this by producing a science, not a philosophy, of history: a science which is, before anything else, conscious of its own problematic and purpose.

Chapter Three

THE HISTORICITY OF KNOWLEDGE

1.1 Man's cognitive relationship with the world

Ibn Khaldun's theoretical analysis establishes that existence is what it means to man, or man's image of it. This stage signifies the perfection of man's ability to think with reference to the existence and possible future contact with the supernatural world.

But supernatural access is an esoteric mission and only Prophets and mystics can undertake it by virtue of secluding themselves from material life, or following certain somato-spiritual exercises. The genesis of knowledge is, then, decided by the development of man's cognitive potentiality in an ascending order (natural, social, historical, philosophical, and metaphysical) accompanied by the enhancement of his cognitive capability.

Ibn Khaldun's classification of the process of acquiring knowledge, in parallel to the worlds of man's existence, into three qualitatively distinctive levels, has a crucial significance in explaining the historicity of philosophical knowledge.

The first kind of knowledge, i.e. perceptions, is based on man's instinctive relation with the natural world. Man's position is analogous to that of the animals, differing only by the fact that man's perceptions initiate his action; and he uses his discerning mind to plan his action according to a desired end. (We will speak about this point later) once he acts to achieve his basic ends, the satisfaction of his livelihood, he needs the cooperation of other men and enters into mutual (communal) relationship with them. This leads to fundamental transformations in his knowledge: within his experience of social life he can test what he has learnt, emphasize what is useful and right for him, and fix them in his mind as concepts. It is only after undergoing this experimental stage that mind is able to realize the essence of things and work out abstract and hypothesize knowledge. It follows that, philosophy itself is the product of man's practical involvement in the world, and his social existence. It is not idea that determines history, but it his history in terms of man/reality as a relationship, that generates ideas and transforms them according to the vicissitudes of this qualitative relationship.

By formulating this materialist concept of history Ibn Khaldun does not antagonise the idea of the supernatural. He recognizes the existence of the supernatural world as an established fact that we deduce from the influence that it exercises upon us. But as far as man is concerned, the only empirical proof for the existence of the supernatural world is

> "confused dreams", which are "pictures of the imagination that are stored inside by perception and to which the ability to think is applied after (man) has retired from sense perception." (v.II p. 420).

Beyond this proof, Ibn Khaldun argues, the conjectures of the metaphysicians about details concerning the essences of the spiritual world and their order is dubious, "because the conditions of logical argumentation do not apply to them" (V. II p. 120) as they are of an unknown essentiality. This means that these essences are theory-refutable, as they are not reachable by the range of our "physical observation". In other words the supernatural world is existent to us to such an extent that it can be reflected in our thinking.

To assert the reconciliatory aspect of his philosophy, Ibn Khaldun tries to conceptualise his argument within the Quranic context. Thus he authorizes a general definition he gives to thinking ability by inferring it from Quranic verses:

> "The ability to think is the occupation with pictures that are beyond sense perception, and the application of mind to them for analysing and synthesis. This is what is meant by the word of afidah "heart" in the Quran. He gives you hearing and vision and hearts. (16; 78) Afidah, "hearts", is the plural of fuad. It means here the ability to think." (V. 2 p. 412)"

1.2 The necessity of principles for understanding history.

In the foregoing argument we have tried to explicate Ibn Khaldun's answer to the question: where do principles come from? And now we should answer another question: Why are principles necessary for man?

According to Ibn Khaldun, principles are necessary for man because his actions are not, like animals, extemporary. They are intentional and directed towards a specific goal.

Before embarking on his work, man conceives the plan he will follow and the end he will achieve. By giving man the ability to think, "God caused him to act in an orderly and well arranged manner", and enabled him thereby to control the whole world of things.

"Everything is subservient to man and works for him. This is meant by the 'Appointing of a representative mentioned in the Quran: 'I am appointing a representative on earth." (V. II, p. 416)

Thus, Ibn Khaldun relates the disciplined actions of man not only to reason, but also to the concept of Istikklaf. This means that man is not only a philosophical potentiality, but a political agent as well. He uses his hands and creates his own world, and his own system of existence. For this purpose, he needs knowledge; he needs guiding principles.

"Therefore, the political is primary, and the philosophical is ancillary. Here, both reason and action (i.e. philosophy, politics and history) integrate within the enterprise of Istikhlaf:

> "He (God) enabled them (human beings) to arrange for (their activities) under political aspects and according to philosophical norms. Those (political aspects and according to philosophical norms) lead human beings from the things that are detrimental (to them), to those that are in their interests, and from evil to the good." (V. 2 p. 418).

Thus, the act of reconciliation ends by superseding religion by philosophy within the concept of Istikhlaf and exteriorising it as extra-historical potentiality.

This secular attitude of Ibn Khaldun is explicitly expressed in his reputation of the theological dimension of Aristotelian philosophy, based on a monist view referring all existentia to the first intellect. According to Ibn Khaldun,

> "This means that they disregard all the degrees of divine creation beyond the (first intellect). Existence, however, is too wide to (be explained by so narrow a view). And He creates what you do not know." (V. III p. 256)

No doubt that this break with Aristotlianism is inspired, at this point, by the spirit of the Quranic discourse which behoves man to understand creation in its width, and variety. To convince us of this fact, Ibn Khaldun annotates his afore-mentioned argument with a Quranic verse.

So far, we can say that Ibn Khaldun builds his science of history on his extrapolation of philosophical principles from the universal aspects of the Quranic discourse and Greek philosophy, especially, Aristotle's (see p. 248 V. III – 250).

To conclude, Ibn Khaldun's philosophical concept of the world is both metahistorical and historical. But the metahistorical principles do not detach themselves from the conditions of human reality. They are located within the nexus of those conditions on the basis of the materiality of human existence: which is the principle of principles in Ibn Khaldun's philosophy. That is why Ibn Khaldun's principles are logical (methodological) and concrete; conceptual and phenomenal. It is this realistic understanding of the notion of principle that allows Ibn Khaldun to his New Science within the space that distances the concrete from the conceptual: the distance of human action. Viewing man and his society as parts of a single material world, he made the first methodological attempt in history to develop a theory of social development by applying the principles of political philosophy and the analogical regime on which the positive sciences are based, to the study of human civilization. Thus, in order to become a science, history, like any other science, had to take an "inductive leap, occupying a new vantage ground from which it can see former data as new things to be explained."

Chapter Four

KNOWLEDGE AND METHOD: THE QUESTION OF TRUTH

4.1 The meanings of history

In his search for truth Ibn Khaldun starts out by drawing a structural distinction between two meaning of history and consequently two kinds of knowledge.

1. The "surface meaning" of history – or the surface knowledge.
2. The "inner meaning" of history – or the deep knowledge.

The surface meaning of history includes all historical information, which harbours or conveys "untruth" or "outward truth". It is presented in a narrative form, which masquerades its "untruth". Ibn Khaldun says:

> "On the surface history is no more than information about political events, dynasties and occurrences of the remote past, elegantly presented and spiced with proverbs."(M. I. p. 6)

This surface information consists of a large number of gossips, discredited reports, nonsensical stories, fables, myths, bizarre exaggerations, superstitions and hearsays. It is riddled with errors and unfounded assumptions.

The "inner meaning of history" constitutes that kind of knowledge which:

> "Involves speculation and an attempt to get at the truth, subtle explanation to the causes and origins of the existing things, and deep knowledge of the how and why of events." (p. 6) It is this search for deep knowledge, this quest for truth, which makes history, as Ibn Khaldun sees it, "firmly rooted in philosophy", a reality, which makes it (history) "deserve to be accounted a branch of philosophy."(V. I p.6).

And he describes his own theory in Al-Muqaddima as: "turn-(ing) out to be a vessel for philosophy, a receptacle for historical knowledge." (p.12).

But Ibn Khaldun realizes that before reaching the truth, one must traverse many stations of error; observing, and trying to understand the conditions that make "untruth" possible. Why is "untruth" hardly avoidable in historical discourse? A network of subjective and objective reasons is responsible for not only making the "surface knowledge" possible, but also unavoidable and prevailing.

In terms of pure scholarship, Ibn Khaldun distinguishes these three conditions:

- Lack of originality and critical insight in dealing with the events;
- The influence of tradition and dogma. "Blind trust in tradition is an inherited trait in human beings." (V. I p.7)
- The nature of scholarship and its position within the institutational discipline of the existent political system.

To explain these reasons, Ibn Khaldun begins his book with a general survey of the shortcomings of the previous historians.

4.2 Errors of traditional historians

He presents a large number of their "errors" and conducts a masterly logical discussion about the nature and reasons of these errors. He is constantly aware of approaching each historian in the context of his time and place. He argues that the works of the first group of historians such as al-Masudi, al-Wagidi, Ibn-Hayyan and Ibn-al-Ragig were characteristic of their originality. The serious shortcomings which, however, can be found in their works, were the natural outcome of the historical conditions in which they lived and their lack of a philosophical insight into the nature of life. Nonetheless these works are still valuable. They "have been distinguished by universal acceptance of the information they contain and by adoption of their methods and their presentation of the material".

So, they are original on both their method and their material. But Ibn Khaldun argues,

> "later historians were all tradition-bound and dull of nature and intelligence...they merely copied the older historians and followed their example." (V. I p. 4).

But traditions are not in itself a serious fault. In fact, it is corollary to a serious gap in the historian's thinking, which is, "disregard (of) the changes in conditions and in the costumes of nation and races that the passing of time has brought about." (p.9).

4.3 Change of concepts and definitions

Ibn Khaldun firmly believes that with the passing of time everything in life changes:

The people' ways of making a living, their customs, their institutions and attitudes of life, their concept, etc... He conducts a logical argument to show how even such concepts as "scholarship" – teaching, and "jurisprudence", had by his time attained new meanings, different from those in the Beginning of Islam when scholarship meant the transmission of statements people had heard the Lawgiver (Muhammad) make. So scholarship was essentially teaching the laws of Islam as a religious mission, "not as one gives professional instruction". Persons "of noble descent" and companions of Muhammad himself undertook the mission of teaching the Book of God and the Sunnah of the prophet. But when the Islamic community transferred from "Badawa" (desert life) to "civilization", and the State of Islam expanded in the East and West, the "division of labour" appeared and scholarship was no longer an integral part of the political and spiritual task and practice of the rulers. The statesmen dedicated themselves to the administrative affairs of royal and governmental authority. The cultivation of scholarship was entrusted to others.

Gradually, it became a craft that served as a mode of living; but became corrupt when teachers working for a living took on the task without being fit for it.

In the same way, Ibn Khaldun explains the changes which the concept if "jurisprudence" had undergone.

Thus, according to Ibn Khaldun, all the changes that occur in a society are due to the development of social organization, which in its turn depends upon the changing modes of making a living. The mutation of concept becomes increasingly apparent when crafts and specialization appear. But Ibn Khaldun argues that the historians could not detect this fact; therefore, their conception of history remained old fashioned and traditional. They were not aware that even one's point of concern in history, and consequently the object of historiography should change according to the vicissitudes of social reality. One of the methods of historical writing was, for instance, to record the genealogy of dynasties and biographical details about the rulers, such as mentioning the name of each ruler, his ancestors, his parents, his wives, his surname, his seal ring, his judge, his door-keeper and wazir. This procedure Ibn Khaldun remarks was followed by the historians of the Ummayid and Abbasid dynasties, when this method had as its political justification:

> "The purpose of writing for members of the ruling dynasties, whose children wanted to know the lives and

circumstances of their ancestors, so that they might be able to follow their steps and what they did."

So, this method was justified by an epoch when the ruler as an absolute authority stood in the centre of historical significance. But by Ibn Khaldun's time the historical concern. Now "historical interests was concentrated on the rulers themselves and the mutual relationship of various dynasties in respect to power and predominance. The problem now was which nations could stand up and which were too weak to do so."

Thus, historical process had brought forth new problems and the historical concern no more the family life of the rulers but the question of the very survival of nations in the context of power struggle and national domination. Therefore, maintaining the genealogical narrative meant nothing but mere blind imitation of former authors and in doing so the historians distorted the broad image of reality and reduced the range of historical knowledge to trivial details and, and the same time, robbed the methodology of the early historians of the value of its originality.

Historian's subjective approach to history Ibn Khaldun is against this travesty because it disregards the intention of former authors and tramples on the purpose of historiography. How does the intention of a historian or a reporter decide the nature of historical information?

To Ibn Khaldun the contribution of a reporter's subjectivity to making of "untruth" unfolds itself in different phenomena:

1. Partisanship for schools, sect and opinions. That is to say ideological, social or intellectual partisanships prompt the historians to transmit the information that conforms to their biases and reject the rest. Therefore, "partisanship" and prejudice obscure the critical faculty and preclude critical investigation. The result is that falsehoods are accepted and transmitted." (V. I p. 71)
2. The historian's lack of intellectuality, which results in his ignorance of the nature of his career, and the authentic value of the items of information which he obtains. He may copy what transmitters say

"It is the story of an alleged copper city...in the desert of Silimash which Musa bi Nusayr crossed on his raid against the Maghreb...etc."

Before Ibn Khaldun Islamic histories were padded with such fictions. The historians avoided investigating their truth. It was Ibn Khaldun's genius, which initiated the analytical method of dismantling such superstitions. About "the Copper City" he says:

> "All this is an absurd story. It belongs to the idle talk of storytellers.
>
> Travellers and guides have crossed the desert of Silmash. They have not come across any information about such a city. All the details mentioned about it are absurd (if compared with) the customary state of affairs.
>
> They contradict the natural facts that apply to the building and planning of cities. Metal exists at best in quantities sufficient for utensils and furnishings. It is really absurd and unlikely that there would be enough to cover a city with it."(V. I p. 76)

Then, what is to be done? How can our critical investigation rid historical discourse from falsehood? Ibn Khaldun's response is clear. Critical philosophy must establish history as a science by distancing fiction from historical knowledge and thus providing an epistemological space for history's scientific construction. In other words, in order that historiography would become a science it must constitute its own object of study, distinguish its boundaries from other related sciences, especially theology and Hadith, tradition, and deploy philosophical principles to establish its methodology, and fulfil its ends. Therefore Inn-Khaldun's main concern is to extricate the object and method of historiography from that of the science of the tradition. According to him, this science is primarily concerned with legal prescriptions and commands to action, and confines itself to authority-criticism in order to find out whether these prescriptions and commandments were actually laid down by the proper authorities. While history is primarily concerned with actual events (Wagi'at), therefore we should criticise statements about events by studying their nature and the conditions of their possibility. In this way history will be allowed to possess its own criteriology of truth. Having defined the subject of history as "a narrative of human aggregation which is the organized habitation - *umran* – of the world" and called his science "the science of *umran*", Ibn Khaldun emphasized the historian's knowledge of the principle of "causation and the conditions of possibility as the fundamental prerequisites of historical writing. To avoid falling into an abyss of errors the historian "Must know the causes of the similarities in certain cases and of differences in others. He must be aware of the different origins and beginnings of different dynasties, and religious groups as well as of reasons and incentives that brought them into being and the circumstances and history of the person who supported them. His goal must be to have complete knowledge of the reason for every happening, and to be acquainted with the origin of every event. Then he must check transmitted information with the basic principles he knows. If it fulfils their requirement, it is sound. Otherwise the historian must consider it as spurious and dispense with it." (V. I p.56). This is the agenda that Ibn Khaldun works out for a science of history.

Although involved in his science is analogy as a method of approach, Ibn Khaldun is aware of the misrepresentations that are concomitant with it. "Analogical reasoning and comparison, he says, are well-Know to human nature but they are not safe from error". They may cause an intellectual to replace the facts of reality by the structures of his own thought, dealing with the vocabularies of his own intellectuality instead of dealing with "living" and ever-changing reality.

Hence, he loses sight of the gap that time has created between the present and the past, and "falls into an abyss of error." (See V. I. P. 58).

Thus historical self-conscious thought attains its perfection by establishing itself as a science. "Such is the purpose of this first book of our work." Ibn Khaldun explains.

"The subject is in a way an independency science. It has its own peculiar object – that is, human civilization and social organization. It also has its own peculiar problems – that is, explaining the conditions that attach themselves to the essence of civilization, one after the other..." (V. I p. 77)

Chapter Five

MAN AND HISTORY: THE QUESTION OF POWER

5.1 Philosophical premises

In German Ideology, Marx and Engels write: "This method of approach is not devoid of premises. It starts out from the real premises and does not abandon them for a moment. Its premises are men, not in any fantastic isolation and rigidity, but in their actual, empirically perceptible process of development under definite conditions." The above description is also applicable to Ibn Khaldun's approach to history. His premises are precisely "men…in their actual, empirically perceptible process of development under definite conditions," i.e.: they are primarily sociological premises formulated on the basis of his philosophical principles; especially of causation which presupposes cognizance of essence, nature and the attached conditions of a thing or a phenomenon. Therefore, to understand Ibn Khaldun's concept of history it is necessary to recapitulate or further elaborate on his philosophical principles regarding man and human action.

1. Man's essence: Man is primarily matter: a clot of blood and a lump of flesh, with God-given potentialities of life, knowledge and meaningful action.
2. Man's nature:
    a. Man is able to develop his ability of thinking and knowing into higher qualitative degrees according to the extent and quality of his actions and experiences in the world. But, generally speaking, man can know his own world only. Ibn Khaldun accepts the limitations put on the range of man's cognizance in the Quran – such as the impossibility of knowing the reality of soul, the appointment of the Day of Judgement, the identify of God, and many secrets concerning Creation.

    b. God has appointed Man as his representative on earth and gave him the ability to organize his actions and live rationally according to the norms of goodness and justice. Man can use his hands, make tools, and produce the means of his sustenance. He can build civilization and transform his life. He can arrange the affairs of his being by depending on himself without any need for divine intervention. Even prophets are not necessary, by logic, for guiding mankind. (V. I p. 93)

    c. Man is capable of aesthetic feeling and creating art. He senses and appreciates beauty in nature and life. "The object in which he is most likely to perceive perfect harmony is the human form." (V. 2 p. 398) Man is also capable of "verbal expression" and the use of writing to communicate his ideas. (See V. III, Chap. 4, Section 33)

    d. There are no racial or ontological distinctions between men and nations by reference to which their identity can be distinguished. Even blood ties and environmental factors do not establish permanent peculiarities of a given nation, because they are subject to change according to the transformation that occurs in the modes of production. (See V. I, p. 173).

"Man is the child of custom, not the child of his ancestors." (V. II, p. 310). And Ibn Khaldun quotes Muhammad as saying *"Every infant is born in the natural state. It is his parents who make him a Jew or a Christian or a Magian."* (V. I, p. 254). Hence, Ibn Khaldun explains that –

"Man is the child of his natural disposition and temperament. The conditions to which he has become accustomed, until they have become for him a quality of character and matters of habits and customs have replaced his natural disposition." (V. I, p. 198)

e. Humanity is a midway position between animality and angelhood. Man may stay in or relegate to the state of animality, behave wildly and devour each other. The power that restrains them from this is reason (which is the meaning of humanity) and/or authority. Man can also elevate to the state of angelicality through abandoning the material mode of his existence. Ibn Khaldun distinguishes prophets as having a particular quality of soul through which they are prepared to have divine knowledge. (V. III, p. 157).

1. The attached conditions: the sum total of the material conditions that make human life possible. God created everything in the heavens and on earth for man and gave it to him. This is indicated, Ibn Khaldun says, in several verses in the Quran. (See V. II p. 311).

The above-mentioned premises further substantiate the main characteristic of Ibn Khaldun's philosophical principles, namely, their materialist foundation. Therefore, they are universal, objective and to a large extent, scientific. But they become subject to limitation once Ibn Khaldun historicizes them in the context of his political thought. Nevertheless, they allow him to place history on its real foundation: the materiality of human existence; from which, Ibn Khaldun derives his dynamic concepts about human civilization, as we are going to explain.

5.2 The Historicization of the World of Existence

Explaining the nature of the "break" Marx achieved in the domain of history, Engels wrote:

> "History for the first time was placed on its real foundation; the obvious fact, hitherto totally neglected, that first of all man must eat, drink, have shelter and clothing and therefore must work, before they can struggle for supremacy and devote themselves to politics, religion, philosophy, etc...this obvious fact at least found historical recognition.

"(Cited in M.H. Bober, Karl Marx's interpretation of history", Fourth edition, Harvard Uni. Press, 1968, p. 4)

Engels, however, was not aware that Ibn Khaldun had not only recognized this obvious fact, but had preceded Marx by five centuries in making it the basic premises of his concept of history. It is this premises that initiates the historicization of his philosophical principles in the context of his science of umran. To Ibn Khaldun, "God created and fashioned man in a form that can live and subsist only with the help of food." (V. I p. 89)

The means of his sustenance are provided in nature, but it requires work and effort. "Thus, to Ibn Khaldun, labour is corollary to man's life. And corollary to labour is human aggregation. Men have to aggregate, to specialize and to produce tools for work and for defending themselves against wild beasts. This human aggregation primarily represents man's instinctive response to a vital necessity, the necessity of survival. From human aggregation the narrative of history starts. But in order that this narrative which is the subject-matter of the science of umran should continue, we need to establish its beginnings (muqaddimat); for, science, as we have explained before, has to have its own logical principles which go into the process of its constitution as a science.

1. The naturally-inspired cooperative inclination of a social group to obtain its basic needs in the context of given concrete conditions of place and time forms what Ibn Khaldun calls: the way of making a living. This is a socio-historical concept, which Ibn Khaldun uses to account for the difference that characterizes the cultural institutions of different nations. It is also, "the way of making a living" that shapes the character, behaviour and the political attitude of the individuals.

2. Because of their God-given privilege of reason, human beings are aware of their need to cooperate and develop a civilized community in which they can share the fruits of their labour. Ibn Khaldun calls this primitive common feeling among the members of a group "Asabiyya". Then develops this term into the most important premise in the context of his science of umran. Asabiyya is primarily linked with man's natural disposition to reflect upon the outcome of things and to conduct a rational mode of being; conditions, which establish his humanity.

3. But, as we have explained in the previous section, men's ability to think is not an absolute pre-given condition. It is a developing state, which involves qualitative transformations. This means "this natural disposition to reflect upon the structure of things, which is the real meaning of humanity, exists, among men in different degrees." (V. II p.357). It follows that all the members of a group, by necessity, do not have equal levels of humanity or mental awareness. Many of them may still be in the state of animality, prepared to be aggressive and destroy the cooperative structure of social organization. Therefore, reason as such, i.e.: humanity must be buttressed by a more effective restraining power, which is "authority". And this authority is to be exercised by one of the members of the group, a ruler. Therefore, the existence of a ruling power is more essential to the possibility of social organization than reason as such. Hence, the establishment of royal authority (mulk) is, according to Ibn Khaldun "a natural quality of man which is absolutely necessary to mankind, to prevent them from devouring each other." (V. I p. 92). To sum up, it is power that replaces reason in accounting for the possibility of human civilization.

4. Mulk cannot exist without its power structure, which is asabiyya. It is asabiyya that leads to the emergence and establishment of mulk, royal authority, and sustains it. The strength of mulk and the range of its expansion are contingent on the power of its asabiyya. But asabiyya in its turn is not an abstract power structure. It is shaped and conditioned by the concomitant modes of production.

5. "The real meaning of mulk, Ibn Khaldun argues, " is that it is a form of organization necessary to mankind"; but mulk as such cannot safeguard the perpetuation of human civilization (which is almost a synonym to the state itself). According to Ibn Khaldun, "mulk requires superiority and force which express the wrathfulness and animality of human nature. That is to say, mulk, which essentially came into existence in order to protect mankind from anarchy and destruction, is itself liable to reverse to animality and become an instrument of despotism and corruption. Therefore, it is necessary that mulk should be rational and have reference to ordained philosophical and political norms, which correspond to the principles of justice and legitimate leadership.

Within the theoretical framework already expounded, Ibn Khaldun problematizes history as the question of the State, its rise and decline within the context of conflict between reason, authority, and asabiyya. He establishes asabiyya as the dynamic force in history and the development of any political system. The dynamism of asabiyya lies in its dialectical relation with the modes of production; a characteristic, which allows, although to a limited extent, the historicization of the concept of the State. In the following we shall try to investigate the nature and role of asabiyya both as a historical concept, i.e.: in its relation with labour and modes of production, and as an abstract concept; i.e.: in its relation to power.

5.3 Asabiyya and Umran

- Man's cooperative labour in response to the natural necessity of his survival leads to the establishment of umran, habitation (or urbanisation). The primary cause that dominates the direction and development of umran is asabiyya. Historically speaking asabiyya exists primarily as a potency lying in the genealogical centre of small group possessing only the bare necessities of their life. What strengthens asabiyya in this stage is men's fear of external danger or the threat of other asabiyya-groups. Therefore, it is natural that the first form of asabiyya should be based on consanguinity, which conforms to the clan structure of their way of making a living. (See V. I, Chap. 2, Section 8)

- Asabiyya enables the population of an umran to cooperate towards making their livelihood. They start with the bare necessities of life: food, clothing and shelter; depending on agriculture, hunting, animal husbandry, etc. This mode of life forms Badawa, or umrani badawi, Bedouin urbanisation, which comprises both nomadic and agricultural societies characterized by natural livelihood.
- The main historical change that occurs in human society, according to Ibn Khaldun is its transition from badawa to hadhara, civilization. This transition depends on transformations that take place in the economical structure of umrani badawi. Primitive cooperative labour leads to the increase of production and the size of the population of umran. Where population increases, a large amount of labour then, is channelled towards the production of things and the provision of services that are rather superfluous. This creates prosperity and in its turn leads to higher demographic fertility. From now on surplus labour is used as a source of profit.

"It is spent to provide the conditions and customs of luxury and to satisfy the needs of the inhabitants of other cities. They import (the things they need) from (people who have a surplus) through exchange or purchase. Thus the people who have a surplus get a good deal of wealth." (V. 2 p.272).

This state of prosperity and wealth results in two important factors: the accumulation of capital and the increase in the rate of consumption. These two factors in conjunction with the surplus manpower lead to the cultivation of crafts. Moreover, the desire to acquire profit prompts the craftsmen and skilled persons to compete over the arising demand for luxuries and consequently for the quality of their products. Furthermore, practice furthers their intelligence and skill. As a result, industry and crafts thrive, and the division of labour is consummated between agriculture on the one hand, and commerce and industry on the other, establishing two totally different modes of life: rural and urban. Once this stage in the development of civilization is reached, man is able to develop the sciences although they do not produce any immediate gain, nonetheless, constitute fulfilment of mankind's higher aspiration in the domains of the spirit and the intellect. "Because man's ability to think desires to obtain perceptions that it does not yet possess." (Vol. II, p. 412)

The above argument demonstrates that labour constitutes the infrastructure of social transmutations. But Ibn Khaldun argues that labour can lead to the development of human civilization only through its subservience to power. Its man's will to power that lies behind the whole process of civilization, which is concurrent with the development of the State.

How does Ibn Khaldun account for this thesis? Natural necessity generates the first human assemblages, the first form of asabiyya based on consanguinity and "mutual affection and willingness to fight and die for each other." (vol. I, p. 313)

This asabiyya gives the group both "aggressive and defensive strength". In the stage of badawa, the group is content with the bare necessities of life and its main concern is to remain coherent. For this purpose it needs a dominating element. Hence, asabiyya expresses itself in the form of legitimatising the restraining power of a person among the group, giving him mulk, royal authority. Mulk and domination, then, are implicit within asabiyya as its telos. This fact is materialized once the group is urbanised.

"Now, royal authority is a noble and enjoyable position. It comprises all the good things of the world, the pleasures of the body and the joys of the soul. Therefore, there is, as a rule, a great competition for it. It rarely is handed over (voluntarily), but it may be taken away. Thus, discord ensues. It leads to war and fighting and it attempts to gate superiority. Nothing of all this comes about except through group feeling (asabiyya)." (V. I p. 313)

Asabiyya establishes the power structure of royal authority through safeguarding the group's submission, consent and sacrifice. This creates a favourable position for the ruler to achieve his hegemony over his own group in the first place, and then to extend his domination by force over other groups. Gradually, the elements of blood ties lose their significance and are replaced by power as an abstract element. For the small individual asabiyya-groups abandon or modify their pedigree to establish affiliations with the dominating power, and are incorporated within its asabiyya to form a single great asabiyya, i.e. dawla, the state, which is the consummated form of mulk.

Thus, Asabiyya gives a group the superiority without which royal authority cannot be achieved. At the same time, by making social organization possible, it establishes the first condition of umran. And historical evolution, the transition from Badawa to sedentary culture, is concurrent with the transformation of royal authority into a fully developed state. In this sense, civilization is no more than the manifestation of the function and reality of the State.

Ibn Khaldun bases this thesis on the following argumentation:

1. Royal authorities establish order and stability and thereby "cause the people to seek tranquillity, restfulness and relaxation, and try to provide the aspects of civilization that were lacking in the desert." This leads to prolificness and, consequently, the increase of surplus labour and production.
2. The elements of sedentary culture are proportionate to the size of royal authority. "For sedentary culture is the consequence of luxury; luxury is the consequence of wealth and prosperity; and wealth and prosperity are the consequence of royal authority and related to the extent of (territorial) possessions which the people of a particular dynasty have gained." (V. I, p. 351)

3. The rulers' proclivity for worldly glory and personal supremacy leads to the prevalence of luxury, conspicuous consumption and prodigality which necessitate the encouragement of crafts and industry on the one hand, and the development of sophisticated cultural institutions such as hospitality, wedding, costume, art and music, etc. on the other.
4. In order to defend it against the attacks of rival asabiyya-groups, a dynasty must plan and build defendable cities and towns with necessary garrisons, towers and fortresses. This gives birth to the building of cities. "Dynasties and royal authority are absolutely necessary for the building of cities and the planning of towns." (V. 2, p. 235)
5. The civilizing role of the state unfolds itself mainly in the fact that it is only the state, which is capable of providing all the necessary means of production; namely, labour, capital, machinery and engineering skill. Some constructions such as cities and monuments can materialize only when there are thousands of workers and united action and cooperation. It is only royal authority, which can enforce the necessary manpower for such projects and bring it together from all sides and regions. (V. I, p. 356)
6. The cultural identity of any nation is contingent upon its entity as a state. Once a nation loses royal authority, it simultaneously loses its national identity, language and cultural characteristics. In discussing this proposition, Ibn Khaldun propounds significant theses with regard to what we may call 'the psychology of the colonizer/the-colonized relationship.' Ibn Khaldun considers it a psychological fact of human nature that " the soul always sees perfection in the person who is superior to it and to whom it is subservient."

Starting from this premises, Ibn Khaldun gives two reasons as to why the conquered imitates the conqueror:\

a. The conquered nation fails to understand and estimate the material consequences of its defeat; therefore it "erroneously assumes that its own subservience (to the conqueror) is not due to the nature of the defeat but to the perfection of the victor. If that erroneous assumption fixes itself in the soul, it becomes a firm belief. The soul then adopts all the manners of the victor and assimilates itself to him." (Section 22; Chap. 2 V. I)

b. The defeated nation, again erroneously, attributes its defeat to the cultural superiority of the dominating nation, thinking that "the superiority of the victor is not the result of his asabiyya or great fortitude, but his customs and manners." Therefore, "the vanquished can always be observed to assimilate themselves to the victor in the use and style of dress, and weapons, indeed, in everything." (V. I, p 299).

Ibn Khaldun especially emphasizes that conquered/colonized nations are forced to abandon their native languages and learn the language of the dominating nation. (Section 22, Chap. 4, V. 2).

The psychological effect of defeatism goes so far that the dominated people recreate the cultural aspects of the dominating nation in their own artistic activities. (See V. I, p. 300).

Presumably, Ibn Khaldun is the first thinker to compare the docile character of the colonized to that of children and to establish the assumption that they try to identify themselves with their rulers. "The ruler dominates those under him. His subjects imitate him, because they see perfection in him, exactly as children imitate their parents or students their teachers." (V. I, p. 300)

Ibn Khaldun does not forget to support his argument with the Quran verse, "The common people follow the religion of their rulers", expressing the fact that the dominating modes of thought and behaviour in any society represent the ideology of the ruling class. But the psychology of the relationship between the colonizer and the colonized takes a very different coloration and direction when a nation, which has historically been proud of its superiority in the domains of power and civilization, is over-powered by another savage or inferior nation. In this case, having lost its freedom and pride, the dominated nation suffers from a deadly spiritual shock. Apathy and pessimism prevail. Under the impact of defeat, asabiyya disappears, civilization diminishes and business and other social activities come to standstill. People become apathetic even down to such matters as food and drink, and propagation. (Even the beasts of prey do not cohabit when they are in human captivity.) As a result, the nation continues to weaken and disintegrate until it perishes. (Section 23, Chap. 2, Vol.I). A historical example of this case, according to Ibn Khaldun, is the disintegration of the Persians under the domination of the Arabs. (See V. I, p. 301)

All the afore-mentioned arguments lead to one conclusion:

It is the question of power, which establishes itself as the object of historiography. Civilization is pre-conditioned and determined by power struggle. Those nations that fail to win superiority and form states have no locus in historical narrative. Once others overpower a nation, it automatically loses its cultural identity and historical role. It will be even robbed of its previous history and cultural achievements. Therefore, the universal question that the science of umran must account for now is: the decline of nations.

Chapter Six

ASABIYYA AND THE DECLINE OF THE STATE.

6.1 Elements of asabiyya

It is natural that the concept of asabiyya should posses the same central position in the aetiology of the decline of the state as it does in the aetiology of its formation. Primarily, asabiyya represents the context of human co-existence: Not the co-existence of human being as such, but of the members of a specific group in a specific place and time. Therefore, by its nature, asabiyya is exclusive, defensive and, at the same time, aggressive. Its origin lies in man's instinctive feeling for self-preservation and, to use an expression from Vico, "tyranny of self-love".

It embodies egoistic interests and will to power of a certain group. Asabiyya always belongs to a group; and there are always many asabiyya-groups, who naturally struggle with one another for superiority and political domination. This is the fundamental characteristic of asabiyya that does not only make it historical, but also the sole historicizing force in existence. (In the sense that history is but the manifestation of man's ever persisting search for survival and will to power.)

As a historicizing power nucleus, asabiyya can be analysed into four elements:

1. Common cause,
2. Common action,
3. Common consciousness and
4. Common obedience to a ruler, i.e. a restraining power.

What gives unity and coherence to these elements is a restraining power exercised by a dominating element, which is the royal authority. In badawa period, all these elements are integrated into one whole, characterized by unity of structure and harmony of action and purpose. But asabiyya in this stage is pre-historical, because rulership, i.e., the relation between the ruler and the asabiyya-group, takes the form of riasa, chieftainship, in which no restraining power is exercised.

The leader has no superiority. He is one of the group, sharing all their sufferings and successes. "He is obeyed but he has no power to force others to accept his rulings". (V. I, p.284).

Asabiyya becomes historical only when it moves towards superiority and gaining royal domination. That is to say when it gives the ruler sufficient power to "rule by force". Therefore, although royal authority is the goal of every asabiyya, not necessarily ever asabiyya has royal authority.

"Royal authority, in reality, belongs only to those who dominate subjects, collect taxes, send out (military) expeditions, protect the frontier regions, and have no one over them who is stronger, than they. This is generally accepted as the real meaning of royal authority." (V. I, p. 381)

It is obvious that royal authority means the power of the state. According to Ibn Khaldun, the candidature of a leader for royal authority, in the sense mentioned above, depends upon his superiority, and superiority belongs to someone who possesses a house and leadership among the tribes.

"A house means that a man counts noble and famous men among his forebears." On this basis, a man is "singled out as leader of all various asabiyyas because he is superior to them by birth." (V. I, p. 337)

As long as a "house" is able to maintain its power to rule by force, royal authority remains exclusively within its genealogical line. But it happens when a house loses its power base, yet people will continue to obey them and accept their royal authority because, in the course of time, their "material superiority" has been established as a theocratic or a hereditary reality whose concrete origins have been forgotten. (See: Section 2, Chap. 3, V. I).

To conclude, Ibn Khaldun's power politics, as we have seen, is established in the context of asabiyya, i.e. the politics of clans, a feudal political regime which relies on two kinds of socio-political relationships:

- an internal one, between the ruler and his own asabiyya.
- an outer one, between the ruling asabiyya and other groups or people in general.

Hence, we have to look for the causes of the decline of the state in the socio-political crises that befall these relationships and give rise to a number of serious contradictions inside asabiyya itself, or in the context of its geopolitical dimensions.

- The contradiction between the centre and the periphery:

The power of asabiyya lies in its genealogical centre. Once it has reached its farthest expansion, asabiyya, which is like the heart that supplies the dynastic territories with vitality, becomes too weak to function properly and its energizing power is necessarily exhausted. The dynasty becomes senile and weak and begins to crumble at its peripheries. Eventually, the centre is destroyed too. In this case, the duration of the dynasty depends upon its numerical strength. If the asabiyya is strong and able to man the outlying regions with its own militia, it will be able to prevent or rather delay the peripheral exhaustion of the dynasty and its

Kamal Mirawdeli

negative effect on central government. (Chap. 3, Section 6, V. I, p. 327-332)

- The contradiction between the ruling asabiyya and divergent or rival asabiyya-groups:
It is easier for asabiyya to control a country with a homogeneous population rather than one with a heterogeneous or tribal make-up. Within the latter the ruling asabiyya has to confront divergent hostile asabiyya-groups, each of which fights for its own common cause.

"At any time, therefore, there is much opposition to a dynasty and rebellion against it." Eventually, the power of dominating asabiyya is exhausted in resisting a series of continual local rebellions. (Chap. 3, Section 8 p. 332-336)

6.2 The internal contradiction between royal authority and asabiyya

a. The natural tendency of royal authority is to attain wealth, glory and power. Once these objectives have been achieved, the ruler, because of the qualities of haughtiness and egoism which are innate in human nature (V. I, p. 337), claims all the wealth and glory, which all the members of the asabiyya-group have sacrificed to obtain as their "common property", for himself. Hence, a serious gap opens up between the ruler and the ruled, on the one hand, and asabiyya breaks up from within on the other. The dominating element can no longer exercise its restraining power in a way that safeguards the coherence of the constituents of Asabiyya. As the ruler excludes his group from possessing property, a common cause will no longer exist. Common consciousness also diminishes. People lose their enthusiasm for common action. ***"They become dispirited and come to love humbleness and servitude"***. Thus, Asabiyya decays and the dynasty suffers from weakness and senility. Eventually it will be over-powered by another strong asabiyya-group.

b. The totalitarianism and egoism of the ruling group brings about a fatal alienation between the dynasty and its asabiyya power structure. Therefore, to preserve dictatorship the ruler seeks military support from outside sources, and recruits mercenaries and hirelings. The financial requirements of this action as well as of the luxurious habits of the ruling men give rise to serious financial problems. The government increases the tax to an extent that people cannot pay. Penalties are imposed on the people and many are deprived of their property…and their affairs of commerce, etc. are weakened, and the latter, in its turn debilitates the regime. (V. I, p. 340). Eventually, the rulers have to reduce the army to the smallest possible size. Hence, the dynasty's military defence weakens and it becomes vulnerable to destruction.

c. The new generations that grow up in comfort and the ease of luxury and tranquillity forget the customs of desert life that enabled them to achieve royal authority and no longer envisage a common motivating cause for action and sacrifice. Therefore, they lose their mobilisation and bravery upon which the power of dynasty relies. Consequently, the dynasty becomes senile and unable to defend itself against enemies. (Chap. 3, Section 11, V. I, p. 339-341).

Ibn Khaldun thinks the decay of dynasties spans the breadth of three generations, as a rule. For dynasties, like individuals, have a natural life span. The first generation retains all the desert visions and qualities of pride, bravery and altruism. Asabiyya is a unified whole with harmonious elements. The negative influences of sedentary culture appear in the second generation. Egoism replaces common cause and common sense. Transition from deprivation to luxury and abundance encourages people to enjoy a lazy life and give up their tribal pride for humble subservience. However, the past still lives in their memory as an illusory reality. They cannot grasp the ideological dimensions of the changes that are taking place in their material life.

"...They live in hope that the conditions that existed in the first generation may come back, or they live under the illusion that those conditions still exist." (V. I, p. 345)

The third generation completely forgets the beginnings. Luxury reaches its peak and social co-existence becomes a sheer illusion. People are dominated by force and robbed of any kind of initiative. They became like women and children and totally dependent on dynasty to defend them. The moral values of desert life retain only symbolic residuals, serving to mystify reality. Asabiyya disintegrates completely and dynasty becomes ripe for decay. (V. I, pp. 344-349).

6.3 ASABIYYA AND BEYOND: THE QUESTION OF CIVILIZATION

Does the aetiological theory of decline leave any space for difference between one civilization and another? Is a meta-asabiyya history possible? Let's consider asabiyya again.

Asabiyya is natural; at the same time it is historical.

The historicity of asabiyya is both initiated and limited by its naturalness. It is not like Hegel's Spirit an absolute, infinite driving force of history, which does not need *"The conditions of an external material of given means from which it may obtain its support, and the object of its activity."*

Asabiyya's growth is contingent on and conditioned by its material ambience. Therefore, as a natural force, it makes history; but, like any other organism, it is exhausted by the history it makes. Asabiyya represents the primitive vigour of man's energy. It expresses man's soul. Yet, it is necessary, because no authority can be established without it. And it is a natural tendency of man to establish royal authority because he is the representative of God on Earth. He needs state to humanize himself, to make rational existence possible for him.

But does asabiyya-state prove this? Ibn Khaldun studies the lessons of Islamic history and comes out with only one lesson, which is history itself. This is "the customary course of affairs", Ibn Khaldun informs us. Human beings ever struggle for power, wealth and political supremacy in a vicious circle of creating and destroying states and civilizations. This is what it is in asabiyya history not what it should be or might be. In order to know what is possible beyond this customary circle, we must have recourse to meta-history: to philosophy and the principles of Sharia' and politics, which inform us that the preservation of the state depends on the nature of rulership itself. Rulership hold is exercised in accordance with philosophical norms and the principles of Sharia in order that social organization might continue despite the disappearance of asabiyya. But Ibn Khaldun emphasizes the fact that only those nations can have rational (we might say democratic) governments, which have really developed into civilized nations and have been able to free themselves from the primitive characteristics of asabiyya politics.

6.4 The case of Arabs

This is an arduous task, which can be achieved only after centuries of experience in building civilization. Furthermore, man's activities in establishing sedentary cultures possible only if environmental factors are facilitating. But this condition has not been available for some nations such as Arabs, whose character and nature, Ibn Khaldun believes, has been shaped by the conditions of desert-life in a way that contradicts the exigencies of civilization and royal authority.

To show Ibn Khaldun's acumen and the originality of his sociological interpretation of the cultural identity of nations, we shall introduce below extracts from his account of the socio-logical dimension of Arab desert life and the cultural implications he derives from them for the interpretation of Arab nationhood.

a. "Savagery has become their [the Arabs'] character and nature. They enjoy it because it means freedom from authority and no subservience to leadership. Such a natural disposition is the negation and antithesis of civilization".

b. "All the customary activities of the Arabs lead to travel and movement. This is the antithesis and the negation of stationeriness, which produces civilization…the very nature of their existence, is the negation of building, which is the basis of civilization."

c. "Labour is the real basis of profit. But the Arabs use force to make craftsmen and professional workers do their work. They do not see any value in it and do not pay them for it. When labour is not appreciated and is done for nothing, the hope for profit vanishes, and no (productive) work is done. The sedentary population disposes, and civilization decays."

d. "Furthermore, (the Arabs) are not concerned with laws…they care only for…looting and imposts. (Therefore), under the rule of (the Arabs) the subjects live as in a state of anarchy without law. Anarchy destroys mankind and ruins civilization, since s we have stated, the existence of royal authority is a natural quality of men."

e. "Because of their savagery, the Arabs are the least willing of nations to subordinate themselves to each other, as they are rude, proud, ambitious, and eager to be the leader…there are numerous authorities and amirs among them. The subject has to obey many masters in connection with the control of taxation and law. Civilization, thus, decays, and is wiped out"…etc. (See sections: 2, 24, 26 and 27 in Chap. 2 V. I, pp. 302-308 and Section 9 Chap. 4 in V. 2).

Thus, although desert life provided Arabs with the great energy and rapacious habits of asabiyya, which made the first stages of dynasties, i.e. the primitive culture, possible, it deprived them of the objective and subject conditions that allow the establishment and development of sedentary culture. They failed to familiarize themselves with the customary activities of civilization, and savagery remained the main anti-cultural characteristic of their life. In this state of affairs, Ibn Khaldun argues, only a meta-historical force, i.e. prophecy, could bring about unity among them and make them inclined to royal authority and civilization.

> "The Arabs attain royal authority once their nature has undergone a complete transformation under the influence of some religious colouring. This is illustrated by the Arab dynasty in Islam. Religion cemented their leadership with the religious law and its ordinances, which, explicitly and implicitly, are concerned with what is good for civilization". (V. I, p. 307)

Religion established a spiritual common cause for various egoistic asabiyya-groups, and thus, served as an extra-historical unifying cohering force. Yet, it did not accomplish this extraordinary task in supernatural manner. Religious Ideology, Ibn Khaldun argues, cannot materialize without asabiyya, which is the necessary requirement of every political enterprise. (V. I, p. 322). Therefore, Ibn Khaldun quotes Muhammad as saying, "God sent no prophet who did not enjoy the protection of his people". The role of religious ideology, then, lies in its significance as a necessary "additional power" that supports the struggle of a powerful asabiyya, the Quaraish in the case of Islam, to overpower those groups that are equal or superior to it in strength. (Section 5, Chap. 3, V. I). Furthermore, according to Ibn Khaldun, religious ideology can materialize only if it conforms with and responds to the material conditions and needs of the life of the society it addresses. Islam was successful not only because Muhammad belonged to a dominating "house" with a powerful asabiyya, (V. I(, p. 404) but also because his teaching were congruent with the desert vision and material reality of the Arabs. Thus, at the beginning, the regime of Caliphate, which was established according to the religious Law, antagonizes royal authority which "as (the early Muslims) saw it, belonged in the same category as luxury and amassed property" (V. I, 421). All the four Caliphs avoided the practices of royal authority:

> "They were strengthened in this attitude by the low standard of living in Islam and the desert outlook of the Arabs. The world and its luxuries were more alien to them than to any other nation, on account of their religion, which inspired asceticism where the good things of life were concerned, and on account of the desert outlook

and habitat and the rude, severe life to which they were accustomed." (V. I, p. 418).

However, Islam enabled the Arabs to establish royal authority and initiate sedentary culture. The primitive strength of their asabiyya helped them to conquer many countries and regions in the East and the West. Arabic being the language of the ruling nation and the Holy Quran, dominated and silenced all other national languages and regional dialects.

At the beginning, however, the Arabs were restricted by religion from *"doing any excessive building or waste (ing) too much money on building activities for no purpose."* (V. 2 p. 268). But after they subjected the Persians and the Byzantine and inherited their civilizations, the tranquillity and luxury they enjoyed led them to building activities and developing all the aspects of sedentary culture. However, the Arabs had no sufficient time to build their own civilization or radically transform their Bedouin nature. For, soon after the expansion of Islam, the regime of Caliphate was no longer capable of responding to the materiality of sedentary culture and had to transform into royal authority. Hence, the rule of religion began to diminish and Arab asabiyya began to suffer from various internal and external contradictions, which eventually led to the decline and destruction of Arab Islamic Empire. Therefore, the Arabs had not enough time to internalise the customary activities and habits of civilization, or objectify their rational skill and creative energy. Thus, once they lost their Islamic domination, they *"neglected the religion"*, forgot political leadership and returned to their desert." (V. I, p. 307).

But "This had no been the case with other nations. The Persians had a period of thousands of years. The same was the case with the Copts, the Nabatacans, and the Somans, as well as of the first Arabs, Ad and Thamud, the Amalekites, and the Tubba's. They had a great deal of time, and the crafts became firmly established among them". (V. 2, pp. 268-269).

Against this background of civilization, we can account for the difference in the systems of government. According to Ibn Khaldun, post-asabiyya history, i.e., the preservation of the state can be possible only if rulership is based on rational (democratic) principles. And rational government, to him, means to have a constitution accepted and respected by people: "It is necessary to have reference to ordained political norms, which are accepted by the mass and to whose laws it submits. The Persians and other nations had such norms. The dynasty that does not have a policy based on such (norms) cannot fully succeed in establishing the supremacy of its rule". (V. I, p. 386).

This suggests that in order to be able to dispense with the asabiyya of one group, the dynasty must procure the asabiyya of people at large. And this can be achieved only if the rule wisely and "democratically" according to philosophically inspired constitutional norms.

We can conclude from Ibn Khaldun's study of the case of Arab identity a number of significant scientific "psycho-sociological" insights into the nature of civilization and the factors that contribute to the shaping of the cultural identity of nations and their modes of existence:

1. The development of civilization depends on objective reality, which, basically, unfolds itself in the environmental conditions of the possibility of human culture. The difference between one nation and other, in terms of superiority, returns to the scope and nature of their cultural achievements, the explanation of which must not refer to any racial or ontological distinctions.
2. Objective reality (for instance, the desert life in the case of the Arabs) shapes the psychological identity of man, which, in its turn, reacts upon the outside world and becomes an essential factor that decides the scope and practicality of the given possibilities of civilization. The relation between man's subjectivity and objective reality is, therefore, dialectic. However, the scope of the transformations that this dialectical relationship brings about is conditioned by the limitations of environmental factors. For example, desert life made savagery the basic characteristic of Arab identity. But savagery, in the sense of love for freedom and movement, and disregard for order and dwelling, turned into a negative factor that resists the possibilities of cultural transformations.

3. As man is a rational being that consciously tries to transform the modes of his existence, his psyche is not exclusively shaped by objective reality. Ideas, also, play a great role in moulding man's psychological identity and reconstructing reality in the minds of people in a way that furthers the possibilities of revolutionary social transformation. But ideas, at the same time, can exercise a negative influence and restrict the tempo of cultural development. This point is substantiated in Ibn Khaldun's illustration of the impact of religion on the identity of the Arabs, and their civilization.

4. Ibn Khaldun's sociological interpretation of identity and civilization stands in opposition to Orientalism, in the ideological sense established by Edward Said, which Western bourgeoisie thinkers and apologists for colonialism have always tried to establish as a scientific concept. For Ibn Khaldun "the reality of humanity" is indivisible. He explicitly rejects rife "erroneous" concepts of his time that the Orientals are superior to Westerners because "the intellect of the people of the East is, general, more perfect than that of the Maghribis [Westerners]." (V. 2, p. 431). Ibn Khaldun explains "superiority" in terms of the conditions and civilization. "The soul grows under the influence of perceptions it receives and the habits accruing to it." (V. 2, p. 433). Hence, the Easterners, to Ibn Khaldun, seemed superior because their soul were "influenced by scientific activity" and sedentary culture had given them much more insight and cleverness" than what Bedouins had. "There is no difference between the East and the West great enough "to be considered a difference in the reality (of human nature), which is one "and the same everywhere." (V. 2. p.431).

5. But, even the advancement of culture and civilization does not, necessarily, mean superiority. In fact, civilization, as a rule, causes the demoralisation of man. Therefore, although sedentary people may be more perfect intellectually, Bedouins are not inferior to them.

"We find Bedouins whose understanding, intellectual perfection, and natural qualifications are of highest rank. The seeming (superiority of) sedentary people are merely the result of a certain polish the crafts and scientific instruction give them." (V. 2, p. 433)

6. In his sociological explanation of the backwardness of Arab civilization, Ibn Khaldun, in fact, designates the fundamental dimensions of the gap that still exists between the Arab world, and all underdeveloped nations on the one hand and develop nations, on the other: a gap which expresses itself in two interdependent realities:

   a. the lack of industrialization (to use a contemporary term in place of Ibn Khaldun's umrani hadhari, sedentary culture) and
   b. rational governments based on democratic constitutions. And still this gap is filled in by asabiyya-politics, which undermines stability and possibilities of social development and democratisation of Arab societies.

In the face of this gap, Arab nationalism still clings to an extreme form of racist nationalism using the Quran and Islam as its main ideology to justify social oppression on the one hand and colonisation of non-Arab nations on the other.

Chapter Seven

EPILOGUE: THE POLITICS OF HISTORICAL THOUGHT

No doubt that all Ibn Khaldun's philosophical, historical and sociological theses, themes and arguments that we have systematically presented and reconstructed in the foregoing sections substantiate our primary hypothesis that his historiography represents first of all a materialist vision of the world. It is this vision that accounts for the universality, objectivity, unusual impartiality and rigorous realism and rationalism that characterize his theoretical discourses. It is also this materialist world vision that makes his concept of history holistic and, from a scientific point of view, invulnerable to any sort of theoretical compartmentalization and structural polarizations. In the Muqaddima there is no sociologism, psychologism or ideologism. But there is sociology, psychology and ideology; all established as hermeneutic theoretical constructs, interconnected, interdependent and originated in their common structure: the material conditions of human co-existence. In the same way, there are no rigid conceptual structures that Ibn Khaldun tries to reify. Even *"Human nature"* itself is not, for Ibn Khaldun, an abstract concept. It is conditioned and shaped by the materiality of its existential location. There are no abstract and eternal cause/effect, subject/object and body/mind dichotomies. But there is the dialectics of human action, socialization and rationalization. Even Ibn

Khaldun's main historical dualism badawa/hadhara does not divide *"the reality of humanity."* It is just a socio-historical condition and process.

But we notice that while his sociological and philosophical insights are allowed free flux in articulating the totality and dialectics of the reality they address, his historical outlook is circumscribed by limitations and closures, which unfold themselves in the pessimism and determinism that characterize his theory of asabiyya-circle. Ibn Khaldun was at the age of forty, coincidentally the same age at which Muhammad received his Revelation, when he decided to seclude political action and reflect on the meaning of history. Political action, for him, had meant his continual attempt to rationalize the rulers and through them the whole society. But as his experiences demonstrated for him the impracticability of this project, he desperately, discarded the role of reason in history (on the contrary to Hegel) and opted for power as the driving force of history in the context of Man's material existence. Therefore, his history is, on the one hand, a justification for inaction, his own pessimism, and, on the other land, a verification of the deterministic role of power in shaping social development. Unlike Muhammad who established the spiritual interpretation of the inevitability of human conflict for power in order to propagate for a religious cause and provide an ideology for action, Ibn Khaldun had recourse to a materialist interpretation of social struggle in order to substantiate his hypothesis that as one royal authority can be established only by destroying another royal authority, history has to be ever confined to a vicious circle of human conflict.

However, it is naïve to think that Ibn Khaldun's concept of history is an immediate reaction to the failures of his political lifetime: Ibn Khaldun's thought was moulded by his own political experiences and intellectual involvement as well as by the spirit of his age. Ibn Khaldun did not invent asabiyya, but discovered it by virtue of his penetrating philosophical insight, which enabled him to grasp the inner structure of social phenomena. Before being a conceptual structure used by Ibn Khaldun to contextualize his historical discourse, asabiyya had been the social structure of political struggle in the Islamic empire since its establishment. Like the Greek historian Polybius, Ibn-KLhaldun's role was to capture this naturally established social structure mentally and recreate and reconstruct it in his historical *"composition"*.

The question, now, is why Ibn Khaldun's historical perspective cannot go beyond the circle of asabiyya although he adopts a materialist view of history. The answer to this question does not lie in his personal experience, but in the spirit of his time and his political thinking. Unlike Marx, Ibn Khaldun neither had at his disposal that immense tradition of the progressive achievements of man's scientific and philosophical thoughts; nor has the spirit of his age, unlike that of Marx, enabled him to see the rise of a new social class powerful enough to challenge the ruling class and change history. The main closure of Ibn Khaldun's conception of change, however, lies in his class vision of history. Ibn Khaldun's own position was within asabiyya not outside it. This is to say, although he had practically extracted himself from the policy of the ruling aristocracy, his political thinking still represented the visions and interests of this class. In Ibn Khaldun's history man thinks, works, produces, culture, builds civilization, creates art; etc…bur does not "change" the history he makes. Historical evolution, transition from rural to urban culture, comes as a result of the structures man is forced to establish for his self-preservation; and not as a result of his free will. This phenomenon in Ibn Khaldun's historiography can be explained in terms of failure of his political thinking to develop a dialectical social interpretation of the phenomenon of the formation of the state. Ibn Khaldun superimposes a metaphysical necessity on the material causation of the emergence of "royal authority" when he accounts for it in terms of a rational necessity sanctioned by God's making man His Representative on earth. This metaphysical dimension of his concept of the state serves to vindicate autocracy (He believes in the absolute authority of One ruler) and, at the same time, to synchronize the historical development of the State.

The ideological class dimension of Ibn Khaldun's political thought unfolds itself explicitly in his concept of power. To him, power and ruling authority are exclusively confined to aristocratic families who have "house" and strong asabiyya that enable them to rule by force and gain tribal hegemony.

Social change, therefore, is possible only in terms of struggle for political domination among ambitious powerful asabiyyas. This struggle is motivated by man's "natural desire for wealth and glory. The other side of this class concept of power is Ibn Khaldun's aristocratic attitude towards the masses: women and common people at large. Women have no historical position or significance in Ibn Khaldun's history. He mentions them, only a few times, as objects of love-poetry and pleasure or examples of weakness and dependency. "They (women) have no power whatever" Ibn Khaldun thinks "Men control their actions." (V. I, p. 402). But of course this was a true statement reflecting the reality of his society and time. However, the closure of historical perspective of his concept of change expresses itself in his attitude towards the revolutionary action of the masses, to the discussion of which he devotes four pages of his Muqaddima. (V.I, pp. 323-327). Ibn Khaldun mentions a number of instances of revolutionary movements launched by "common people" against "unjust rulers".

> "They call for a change in, and prohibition of evil (practices) and for good practices. They hope for a divine reward for what they do. They gain many followers and sympathizers among the great mass of the people.... they take upon themselves to establish the truth." (pp. 323-324).

Yet, Ibn Khaldun does not think that "the great mass of people" has right to revolt against unjust rulers and establishes a new system based on justice and the norms of Sharia because:

> "God had not destined them for such activities as they undertake. He commands such activities to be undertaken only where there exists the power to bring them to successful conclusion." (pp. 323-324).

And this "sufficient" power, according to his previous logic, is embodied exclusively in traditional aristocracies. It is noteworthy that only in association with the role of the masses in history that Ibn Khaldun explicitly resorts to the idea of "predestination". Thus, it is this political logic that constitutes the kernel of his asabiyya circle: common people must stay outside history. But once they break the canon of this logic and try to change "the customary course of matters permitted by God (p.324) Ibn Khaldun thinks

> "It is necessary to take one of the following courses. One may either treat them, if they are insane, or one may punish them either by execution or beatings when they cause trouble or one may ridicule them and treat them as buffoons." (V. I, p. 326).

Thus Ibn Khaldun, though himself abandoned political power, speaks for and on its behalf. According to this logic, no alternative force can or must challenge the ruling aristocracy. Therefore, *"change"* is possible only within the context of the struggle of aristocratic "forces". But as these forces are identical, i.e., they are of the same nature and represent the same class interests and visions; there is no antithesis, and consequently no change. In other words, the exclusion of lower classes as a force of change means that no class antithesis to the ruling power is possible. As a result there is no dialectics of social progress; no change. Here lies the closure, which constitutes the asabiyya-circle

PART II

<u>Note:</u> All the quotations from Ibn Khaldun are from Franz Rosenthal's excellent translation:

<u>The Muqaddima</u> (3 volumes), Princeton university press, 2nd ed. 1967.

I preferred to retain the word "asabiyya" instead of his translation of it as "group feeling"

Footnotes:

(1) Muhsin Mahdi: <u>Ibn Khaldun's philosophy of History</u> p. 26
(2) Northrop Frye: <u>Anatomy of Criticism Princeton, 1957</u>

Bibligraphy

(1) Raymond Aaron: <u>Introduction to the Philosophy of History</u> tr. By. G. J. Irwin, London, 19960
(2) Harry Elmer Barnes: <u>A History of Historical Writing</u> Dover publication, New York 1963
(3) Arthur Marwick: <u>The Nature of history</u> Macmillan, 1970
(4) John H Finley JR.: <u>Thucydides</u> Ann Arbour, 1963
(5) Thucydides: <u>Peloponnesian War</u> tr. By Richard Cravely, every Man's Library, London, 1914. V.I
(6) Herbert Butterfield: <u>Historiography</u> in <u>Dictionary of the History of Ideas</u> New York, 1973. V. 2. Pp. 464-498 (ed. Philip P. Wiener)
(7) Kurt von Fritz: "The Influence of Ideas in Ancient Greek Historiography" in <u>Dictionary of the History of Ideas</u> pp.499-511
(8) Polybius: <u>The Histories</u> tr. By W.R Paton, Harvard University press, 1975. V.i
(9) T.A Sinclair: <u>A History of Greek Political thought</u> 2nd ed. London, 1967
(10) G.W.F. Hegel: <u>The Philosophy of History</u> tr. By J. Sibrec M.A., New York, 1944
(11) E.H. Gombrich: <u>In Search of cultural History</u>, Caledon press, 1969
(12) Arnold Toynbee: <u>A Study of history</u>, Oxford, 1972
(13) Arnold Toynbee: <u>A Study of History</u>, Oxford, 1955. V.3
1. Thucydides, pp. 191-192
2. Polybius, pp. 310-317
3. Ibn Khaldun pp. 321-327

(14) Aristotle: <u>Art of poetry</u>, by w. Hamilton Fyfe, Oxford, 1940
(15) Aristotle: <u>Ethical Nicomachea</u>
(16) Ellen Meiskins wood and Neal wood<u>: Class Ideology and ancient Political theory</u>, Basil Blackwell, Oxford, 1978
(17) Friedrich Meiskins: <u>Historicism</u>, tr. By J.E. Anderson, Rutledge and Kegan Paul, London, 1972. (Voltaire pp. 55-89) (Montesquieu pp. 90-143)
(18) <u>New Encyclopaedia Britannica</u> (1974) v.8 Historiography pp. 945-961 Philosophy of History pp. 961-969
(19) <u>Alan Donavan (ed.):</u> Philosophy of history, Macmillan, 1965
(20) <u>Great Soviet encyclopaedia</u>, Macmillan, 1976 volume 10. History pp. 98-100
(21) Vico: <u>the New Science of Giambattista Vico</u>, tr. By Thomas Goddard Bergin and max Harold Frisch (abridged edition) anchor Books, 1961
(22) Donald Philip Verne: <u>Vico's Science of Imagination</u>, Cornell University press, 1981
(23) Max Harold Frisch and Thomas Goddard Bergin: "the Genesis and Principles of the New Science" in introduction to <u>the Autobiography of Giambattista vico</u>, Cornell University press, New York, 1944 pp. 31-60
(24) R.G. Collingwood: <u>The Idea of history</u>, Oxford, 1962
(25) K. Max, F. Engels, v. Lenin: <u>On Historical Materialism</u> progress publishers, Moscow, 1972
(26) Manfred Behr: "The Greatness and Limitations of classical Bourgeoisie Philosophy, in <u>Soviet studies in Philosophy</u> (A journal of translations) IASP. Vol. XIII, No. 4 Spring 1975
(27) V.I. Lenin: <u>Marx-Engels Marxism</u>, Martin Lawrence, 2nd ed., London, 1931
(28) Karl Marx, Fredrick Engels: <u>The German Ideology</u>, 2nd ed., progress publishers, Moscow. 1968
(29) Robert Daglish (tr): <u>The Fundamentals of Marxist-Leninist philosophy</u>. Progress publishers, Moscow, 1974
(30) Hamilton A.R. Gibb: <u>Studies on the Civilization of Islam</u> Bacon press, Boston, 1962
1. Tarikh pp. 208-134
2. Structure of Religious thought in Islam pp. 176-208

(31) Hamilton A.R. Gibb: "Religion and politics in Christianity and Islam": in <u>Islam and International Relations.</u> (ed) J. Harris, proctor, Pall Mall press, London, 1962 pp. 3-23

(32) <u>Seyyed Hussein Nassr:</u> "Islamic conception of Intellectual life " in <u>Dictionary of the History of Ideas</u>, V. 2, pp. 639-651

(33) Francisco Gabriel: Arabic historiography", tr. From Italian by M.S. Khan in <u>Islamic studies</u> Journal of The Islamic Research Institute, Islamabad, Pakistan. V. XVII, No. 2, Summer 1979, pp. 81-95

(34) Faziur Rahman: "The Quranic Concept of God": In <u>Islamic Studies</u>, Islamic Research Institute, Pakistan, V. 6 1967, pp. 2-25

(35) G. E. Von Grunebaum: Islam: <u>Essays in the Nature and Growth of Cultural Tradition</u>

1. The profile of Muslim civilization pp. 1-17
2. Government in Islam pp. 127-140

(36) Majid Khadduri: "The Islamic Theory of International Relations and its Contemporary Relevance in <u>Islam and International Relations</u>. Pall Mall press, 1962 pp. 24-39

(37) Abdullah Laroui: "The Arabs and History" in <u>The Crisis of the Arab Intellectual</u> University of California press, London, 1976

(38) Sir Muhammad Iqbal: "The Spirit of Muslim Culture" in: <u>Six Lecture on the Reconstruction of Religious Thought in Islam</u>. Labour, 1930, pp. 173-201

(39) Wilfred Cantwell smith: "Islam and History" in <u>Islam in Modern History</u> Princeton University press, 1957, pp. 3-42

(40) Franz Rosenthal: <u>Ibn Khaldun: The Muqaddimah</u> (translated from the Arabic) (The Volumes) Princeton University press, 2nd edition, 1967

(41) Muhsin Mahdi: <u>Ibn Khaldun's Philosophy of History</u> George Allen and Unwin, London, 1957

(42) Aziz Al-Azmeh: <u>Ibn Khaldun: An Essay in reinterpretation</u> Frank Cass, 1982

(43) Aziz Al-Azmeh: <u>Ibn khaldun in Modern Scholarship: A Study in Orientalism</u>, third World Centre for Research and Publishing London, 1981

(44) <u>The New Encyclopaedia Britannic</u> (1974) Ibn Khaldun, V. 9, pp. 147-149

Kamal Mirawdeli

(45) Muhammad Mahmud Rabi: <u>The Political theory of Ibn Khaldun</u> Elden E. J Brill, 1967

(46) Marmaduke Pickthall (tr): <u>The Meaning of the Glorious Koran</u> London, 1930
Muhammad Zafrullat Khan: <u>The Quran</u> (a translation with the Arabic text)

Sources:

1. Ibn Khaldūn. *The Muqaddimah : An introduction to history.* Translated from the Arabic by Franz Rosenthal. 3 vols. New York: Princeton, 2nd edition, 1967.

2. Ibn Khaldūn. *The Muqaddimah : An introduction to history.* Trans. Franz Rosenthal, ed. N.J. Dawood,1967 (Abridged).

Original Sources for thinkers referred to in this book:

1. Hammurabi: The code of Hammurabi, translated by L.W. King
   http://www.sacred-texts.com/ane/ham/index.htm

2. Aristotle:
   Poetics, eritten 350 B.C.E
   Translated by S. H. Butcher. http://classics.mit.edu/Aristotle/poetics.mb.txt
   Politics, written 350 B.C.E, translated by Benjamin Jowett
   http://classics.mit.edu/Aristotle/politics.html
   Nicomachean Ethics, written 350 B.C.E, translated by W. D. Ross
   http://classics.mit.edu/Aristotle/nicomachaen.html

3. **Herodotus: The History of Herodotus**, written 440 B.C.E
   Translated by George Rawlinson

http://classics.mit.edu/Herodotus/history.html

4. **Thucydieds: The History of the Peloponnesian War** Written 431 B.C.E Translated by Richard Crawley
http://classics.mit.edu/Thucydides/pelopwar.html

5. Polybius: **The histories of Polybius. Translated by Evelyn S. Shuckburgh.**
https://archive.org/details/historiesofpolyb02polyuoft

6. Plato:
The Republic, Written 360 B.C.E, Translated by Benjamin Jowett
http://classics.mit.edu/Plato/republic.html
Statesman, written 360 B.C.E, translated by Benjamin Jowett
http://classics.mit.edu/Plato/stateman.html
Symposium, written 360 B.C.E, Translated by Benjamin Jowett

7. Hippocrates: On Airs, Waters, and Places, written 400 B.C.E Translated by Francis Adams
http://classics.mit.edu/Hippocrates/airwatpl.html On Ancient Medicine, written 400 B.C.E, translated by Francis Adams
http://classics.mit.edu/Hippocrates/ancimed.html

8. *St. Augustin's City of God and Christian Doctrine,* **published**: 426 AD translated by Reverend J.F. Shaw
http://oll.libertyfund.org/titles/2053

9. Nicola Machiavelli:
The Prince, translated by Luigi Ricci
http://archive.org/stream/princemac00machuoft/princemac00machuoft_djvu.txt

10. Voltaire
Voltaire, *Toleration and Other Essays* [1755]

http://oll.libertyfund.org/titles/349

Essay on the Customs and the Spirit of the Nations (1756)
http://www.columbia.edu/~pf3/voltaire.pdf

11. Montesquieu: The Spirit of Laws, translated by Thomas Nugent, revised by J. V. Prichard
http://www.constitution.org/cm/sol.htm
http://oll.libertyfund.org/titles/837

12. Ranke: **HISTORY OF THE REFORMATION IN GERMANY. VOL 1-3**

    http://www.cristoraul.com/AUTHORS/Leopold-von-Ranke.html
    http://www.gla.ac.uk/media/media_64280_en.pdf

13. Vico: Philosophy of History

    http://www.revueebook.org/pdf/philosophy-of-giambattista-vico_50ylv.pdf
    http://www.iep.utm.edu/vico/

14. Hegel

    Philosophy of History
    https://www.marxists.org/reference/archive/hegel/hisindex.htm
    Elements of the Philosophy of Right
    http://www.inp.uw.edu.pl/mdsie/Political_Thought/Hegel%20Phil%20of%20Right.pdf

    https://www.marxists.org/reference/archive/hegel/prindex.htm
    Lectures on the History of Philosophy
    https://www.marxists.org/reference/archive/hegel/hpindex.htm

15. Feuerbach:
    Towards a Critique of Hegel's Philosophy, 1839
    The Essence of Christianity, 1841

The Philosophy of the Future, 1843
Lectures on the Essence of Religion, 1851
https://www.marxists.org/reference/archive/feuerbach/

16. Marx:
The German Ideology
https://www.marxists.org/archive/marx/works/1845/german-ideology/
Manifesto of the Communist Party https://www.marxists.org/archive/marx/works/1848/communist-manifesto/
Critique of Hegel's Philosophy of Right 1843
https://www.marxists.org/archive/marx/works/1843/critique-hpr/
Economic and Philosophic Manuscripts of 1844
https://www.marxists.org/archive/marx/works/1844/manuscripts/hegel.htm

17. Marx and Engels:
Complete Marx-Engels Archive
https://www.marxists.org/archive/marx/

18. Marx and Engels on Hegel

ENGELS
Democritus & Epicurus, Marx 1840-41
Schelling & Hegel, Engels 1841
Critique of Hegel's Philosophy of Right, Marx 1843
On the Jewish Question, Marx 1843
Marx's 1844 Manuscripts
Theses on Feuerbach, Marx 1845
The German Ideology, Marx 1845
Method of Political Economy, Marx 1857
Preface to Critique of Political Economy, Marx 1859
Afterword to 2nd German Edition of Capital, Marx 1873

https://www.marxists.org/reference/archive/hegel/li_marx.htm

Islamic Primary Sources

1. The Quran

    Holy Qur'an: Arabic with parallel English translation
    http://www.oneummah.net/quran/
    http://www.almaany.com/quran/?sura=1&aya=1&word_pos=1#.VXCNAM9Viko

2. **Mu'tazilah**

    50 books of al- Mu'tazilah in Arabic:
    http://www.bahzani.net/services/forum/showthread.php?30943-%D9%83%D8%AA%D8%A8-%D8%A7%D9%84%D9%85%D8%B9%D8%AA%D8%B2%D9%84%D8%A9-50-%D9%83%D8%AA%D8%A7%D8%A8

Other sources:

    http://www.philtar.ac.uk/encyclopedia/islam/sunni/mutaz.html
    http://www.islamist-movements.com/25574
    http://www.islamist-movements.com/26404
    http://www.al-tawhed.net/Ferq/ShowCat.aspx?ID=11

3. - Muhammad ibn Jarir al-Tabari طبری

    History of the Prophets and Kings

    The History of the Prophets and Kings is an Arabic historical chronicle
    written by Persian author and historian Muhammad ibn Jarir al-Tabari died 310H from the Creation to AD 915

http://p30download.com/fa/entry/41859/
https://archive.org/details/TarikhTabari_30
http://pdf.tarikhema.org/PDF/%D8%AF%D8%A7%D9%86%D9%84%D9%88%D8%AF-%DA%A9%D8%AA%D8%A7%D8%A8-%D8%AA%D8%A7%D8%B1%DB%8C%D8%AE-%D8%B7%D8%A8%D8%B1%DB%8C/

4. Asharism

https://books.google.co.uk/books?id=9HUDXkJIE3EC&pg=PA280&lpg=PA280&dq=Asharism+Abul-Hasan+al-Ashari&source=bl&ots=XOWoU2glQh&sig=PYn6RyyKITHEf5OIGGqY1QdOkbQ&hl=en&sa=X&ei=d5lwVdPZK4aE7gbe84PQDg&ved=0CEkQ6AEwBw#v=onepage&q =Asharism%20Abul-Hasan%20al-Ashari&f=false
http://www.sunnah.org/aqida/alashaira6.htm

4. ABU AL-HASAN AL-ASH'ARI

Some of his Works

Among al-Ash'ari's books up to the year 320 as listed by himself in *al-'Umad* ("The Supports"):
* *Adab al-Jadal* ("The Etiquette of Disputation").
* *Al-Asma' wa al-Ahkam* ("The Names and the Rulings"), which describes the divergences in the terminology of the scholars and their understanding of the general and the particular.
* *Al-Dafi' li al-Muhadhdhab* ("The Repelling of 'The Emendation'"), a refutation of al-Khalidi's book by that title.
* *Al-Funun* ("The Disciplines"), a refutation of atheists. A second book bearing that title was also written, on the disciplines of *kalâm*.
* *Al-Fusul* ("The Sub-Headings") in twelve volumes, a refutation of the philosophers, perennialists, and members of various religions such as Brahmans, Jews, Christians, and Zoroastrians. It contains

a refutation of Ibn al-Rawandi's claim that the world exists without beginning.

* I*dah al-Burhan fi al-Radd 'ala Ahl al-Zaygh wa al-Tughyan* ("The Clarification of the Proof in the Refutation of Heretics"), a preliminary to *al-Mujaz*.

* *Al-Idrak* ("The Awareness"), on the disciplines that address the subtleties of dialectic theology.

* *Al-Istita'a* ("Potency"), a refutation of the Mu'tazila.

* *Al-Jawabat fi al-Sifat 'an Masa'il Ahl al-Zaygh wa al-Shubuhat* ("The Replies Pertaining to the Attributes On the Questions and Sophistries of Heretics"), al-Ash'ari's largest work, a refutation of all the Mu'tazili doctrines he had upheld previously.

* *Al-Jawhar fi al-Radd 'ala Ahl al-Zaygh wa al-Munkar* ("The Essence: Refutation of the People of Heresy and Transgression").

* *Al-Jism* ("The Body"), a proof of the Mu'tazila's inability to answer essential questions that pertain to corporeality, contrary to *Ahl al-Sunna*.

* *Ithbat al-Qiyas* ("The Upholding of the Principle of Analogy").

* Sessions around the lone-narrator report (*al-khabar al-wâhid*).

* *Mutashabih al-Qur'an* ("The Ambiguities in the Qur'an"), in which he brought together the stands of the Mu'tazila and the atheists in their invalidations of the ambiguities in the hadith.

* *Naqd Ibn al-Rawandi 'ala Ibtal al-Tawatur* ("The Critique of Ibn al-Rawandi's Denial of Mass-Narrated Hadiths"), which contains an affirmation of the principle of Consensus (*ijmâ'*).

* *Naqd al-Mudahat* ("Critique of 'The Similarity'"), a refutation of al-Iskafi on the term *qadar*.

* *Naqd al-Taj 'ala al-Rawandi* ("The Diadem: Critique of Ibn al-Rawandi").

* *Risala ila Ahl al-Thughar* ("Epistle to the People of al-Thughar"), a definition on the doctrines of *Ahl al-Sunna*.

5. al-Farabi, Abu Nasr (*c.*870-950)

Al-Farabi was known to the Arabs as the 'Second Master' (after Aristotle. A philosopher, logician and musician, he was also a major political scientist

al-Farabi (*c.*870-950) *al-Madina al-fadila (The Virtuous City)*, trans. R. Walzer, *Al-Farabi on the Perfect State: Abu Nasr al-Farabi's Mabadi' Ara Ahl al-Madina al-Fadila*, Oxford: Clarendon Press, 1985. (Revised with introduction and commentary by the translator.)

al-Farabi (*c.*870-950) *Risala fi'l-'aql (Epistle on the Intellect)*, ed. M. Bouyges, Beirut: Imprimerie Catholique, 1938. (A seminal text for the understanding of Farabian epistemology.)

al-Farabi (*c.*870-950) *Kitab al-huruf (The Book of Letters)*, ed. M. Mahdi, Beirut: Dar al-Mashriq, 1969. (Modelled on Aristotle's *Metaphysics*, but of interest to students of linguistics as well as of philosophy.)

al-Farabi(*c.* 870-950) *Kitab ihsa' al-'ulum (The Book of the Enumeration of the Sciences)*, ed. and trans. A. González Palencia, *Catálogo de las Ciencias*, Arabic text with Latin and Spanish translation, Madrid: Imprenta y Editorial Maestre, 1953. (A survey of the learned sciences of the day, of encyclopedic range.)

al-Farabi (*c.*870-950) *Kitab al-musiqa al-kabir (The Great Book of Music)*, ed. G.A. Khashab and M.A. al-Hafni, Cairo: Dar al-Katib al-'Arabi, 1967. (Al-Farabi's major contribution to musicology.)

7. Al-Ghazâlî (*c.*1056–1111) was one of the most prominent and influential philosophers, theologians, jurists, and mystics of Sunni Islam.
The Revival of the Religious Sciences (Iḥyā ʿulūm al-dīn)

http://www.ghazali.org/ihya/ihya.htm

- Philosophy and Logic (*falsafa wal manṭiq*): - Click here for more details

    o *al-Muntakhal fi al-jadal*, (The elect in Dialectics) [M:7; A:7; K:13089]
    o *Maqaṣid al-falasifah* (Aims of Philosophers) [M:17; A:16; GAL, I, 425, S., I, 755]
    o *Tahafut al-falasifa* (Incoherence of philosophers). [M:16; A:17; GAL, I, 425, S., I, 754]
    o *Mi'yar al-'ilm fi fan al-manṭiq* (Criterion of Knowledge in the Art of Logic) [M:18; A:18]
    o *Miḥak al-naẓar fi al-manṭiq* (Touchstone of Reasoning in Logic) [M:20; A:20]
    o *al-Maḍnun bihi 'ala ghyar ahlihi* (On the Soul) [M:39; A:39; K:12214, 13243]
    o *al-Qisṭas al-mustaqim* (The Correct Balance) [M:42; A:42; GAL, S., I, 749, no 28]
    o *Ma'arij al-qudus fi madarij ma'rifat al-Nafs* (Ascent to the Divine through the path of self-knowledge) [M:76; A:76; GAL, I, 426 no 64a & 64g, S., I, 751]

8. Ibn Rushd (Averroes)

ABU'L WALID MUHAMMAD (1126-98)

Ibn Rushd (Averroes) is regarded by many as the most important of the Islamic philosophers. A product of twelfth-century Islamic Spain, he set out to integrate Aristotelian philosophy with Islamic thought.

List of works

Some of Ibn Rushd's works are now only extant in Hebrew or Latin, and some not at all. The most useful bibliography is Rosemann, P (1988) 'Ibn Rushd: A Catalogue of Editions and Scholarly Writings from 1821 onwards', *Bulletin de philosophie medievale* 30: 153-215.

Ibn Rushd (1169-98) Commentaries on Aristotle,

Aristotelis opera... cum Averrois Cordubensis vards in eosdem commentariis, Venice: Juntas, 1562-74; repr. Frankfurt: Minerva, 1962. (Ibn Rushd's commentaries as they appeared in Latin and formed part of the approach to Aristotle in Christian Europe.)

- (c.1174) Middle Commentaries on Aristotle, ed. C. Butterworth, *Averroes' Middle Commentaries on Aristotle's Categories and De Interpretatione,* Princeton, NJ: Princeton University Press, 1983. (Translation and commentary on two of Ibn Rushd's major works on philosophical logic and language.)
- (before 1175) Short Commentaries on Aristotle, ed. C. Butterworth, *Averroes' Three Short Commentaries on Aristotle's 'Topics', 'Rhetoric' and 'Poetics',* Albany, NY: State University of New York Press, 1977. (A translation and commentary on three of Ibn Rushd's main discussions of different forms of language.)
- (1179-80) *Fasl al-maqal* (Decisive Treatise), ed. G. Hourani, *Averroes on the Harmony* of *Religion and Philosophy,* London: Luzac, 1961; repr. 1976. (Translation and discussion of the *Fasl al-maqal* and two other short pieces on the same topic.)
- (1180) *Tahafut al-tahafut* (The Incoherence of the Incoherence), ed. S. Van den Bergh, *Averroes' Tahafut al-Tahafut (The Incoherence* of *the Incoherence),* London: Luzac, 1954; repr. 1978. (The standard translation of Ibn Rushd's response to al-Ghazali, incorporating the latter's text.)
- (c.1190) Long Commentary on Aristotle's *Metaphysics,* ed. C. Genequand, *Ibn Rushd's Metaphysics,* Leiden: Brill, 1984. (A

translation and commentary of Ibn Rushd's commentary on Aristotle's *Metaphysics*, Book Lambda.)
- (1194) Middle Commentary on Plato's *Republic*, ed. R. Lerner, *Averroes on Plato's 'Republic'*, Ithaca, NY: Cornell University Press, 1974. (The most modern translation with extensive commentary of Ibn Rushd's commentary on Plato's *Republic.)*

http://www.muslimphilosophy.com/ir/art/ibn%20rushd-rep.htm
http://www.ghazali.org/site/oeuvre.htm

Made in the USA
Monee, IL
26 January 2021